TIME TEAM 97

THE SITE REPORTS

WRITTEN BY TIM TAYLOR, SERIES PRODUCER
ARCHAEOLOGICAL CONSULTANT: MICK ASTON

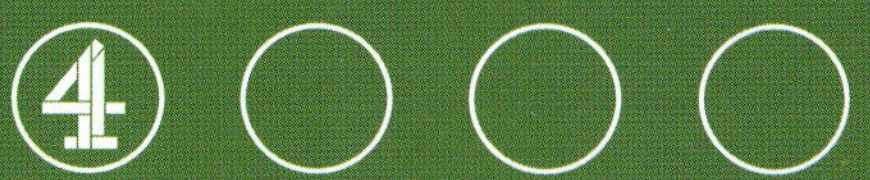

CONTENTS

THE TIME TEAM

Tony Robinson, the series presenter, is probably best known for his role as Baldrick in *Blackadder* and as the Sheriff of Nottingham in *Maid Marian and Her Merry Men*, which he also wrote. He has a keen interest in history and archaeology – he is president of the Young Archaeologists' Club – and is particularly fascinated by ancient Greece and the biblical lands of the Middle East.

Mick Aston, the team leader, has been involved with archaeology for more than 30 years, and is currently Professor of Landscape Archaeology at the University of Bristol. He has written numerous articles and books, including *Interpreting the Landscape*, the standard work on landscape archaeology. To date, he has appeared in five series on archaeology for Channel 4.

Victor Ambrus, a Fellow of the Royal Society of Arts and the Royal Society of Engineers, is a freelance illustrator with more than 250 books to his credit, mostly on historical subjects. He has also designed six sets of historical stamps for the Jersey Post Office and one for the Royal Mail. Winner of the World Wildlife Award and twice winner of the Kate Greenaway gold medal for the best illustrated book of the year, his recent work includes illustrated editions of *The Iliad* and *Moby Dick*.

Robin Bush, formerly Deputy County Archivist for Somerset, is a freelance lecturer, historian and broadcaster. An expert in genealogy and on the history of early emigration to the United States, he is author of numerous books on local history, including a definitive guide to Somerset.

Phil Harding still works as a field archaeologist with Wessex Archaeology, and has been involved in a project listing and plotting all known Palaeolithic sites in Britain. He has also completed a number of excavation reports – including some for TIME TEAM – on sites ranging from the Palaeolithic to the Industrial Revolution. He continues to demonstrate flint knapping at craft shows and to local societies.

Carenza Lewis has been a field archaeologist for the Royal Commission on the Historical Monuments of England for over ten years. A specialist in the medieval period and in historic landscapes, she has worked extensively in Wessex and co-edited a collection of essays on the medieval landscape of this part of England. Her book on the medieval landscape of the East Midlands is to be published in 1997.

Other key members of the team

Stewart Ainsworth trained as a surveyor before moving into the archaeology section of the Ordnance Survey as an investigator, working in Britain on archaeological sites and monuments and, on secondment, on a mapping project on the Caribbean islands of St Kitts and Nevis. In 1985, he joined the Royal Commission on the Historical Monuments of England as an archaeological investigator and is now head of the field archaeology office for the West Midlands.

John Gater has been involved in archaeological geophysics for 17 years, working for British Gas, the Ancient Monuments Laboratory (English Heritage) and Bradford University Research. In 1986, he set up Geophysical Surveys, an independent consultancy in geophysics for archaeology. He is also associate editor of the *Journal of Archaeological Prospection.*

Chris Gaffney has worked in geophysics for over 13 years, including extensive site-based experience in the UK, Greece and the former Yugoslavia. In 1989, he formed a partnership with John Gater at Geophysical Surveys. He, too, is an associate editor of the *Journal of Archaeological Prospection.*

The TIME TEAM (left to right): Tony Robinson, Victor Ambrus, Carenza Lewis. Robin Bush, Phil Harding and Mick Aston,

ST MARY'S CITY

MARYLAND

WHAT MIGHT HAVE HAPPENED

As they stepped ashore in the year of Our Lord 1634, the colonists knew that this was the moment they had been waiting for during the more than four months they had spent at sea. They had faced the threats of disease, pirates and storms and had finally made it to their new home. Here on the shore of the bay the Native Americans called the Chesapeake, they would found a new colony abundant in land and free from the persecution they had experienced in their previous lives.

The reception they received from the local tribes was better than they could have expected. They were welcomed and offered part of a Native American village as shelter, and were shown the riches of the country - the plentiful supplies of fish, oysters, game and maize. A site for the first fort was found, and celebrations were held. The new settlement would be named 'St Mary's' after the Virgin, and if God willed, they would survive and prosper.

Computer reconstruction of St Peter's, the governor's mansion at St Mary's City.

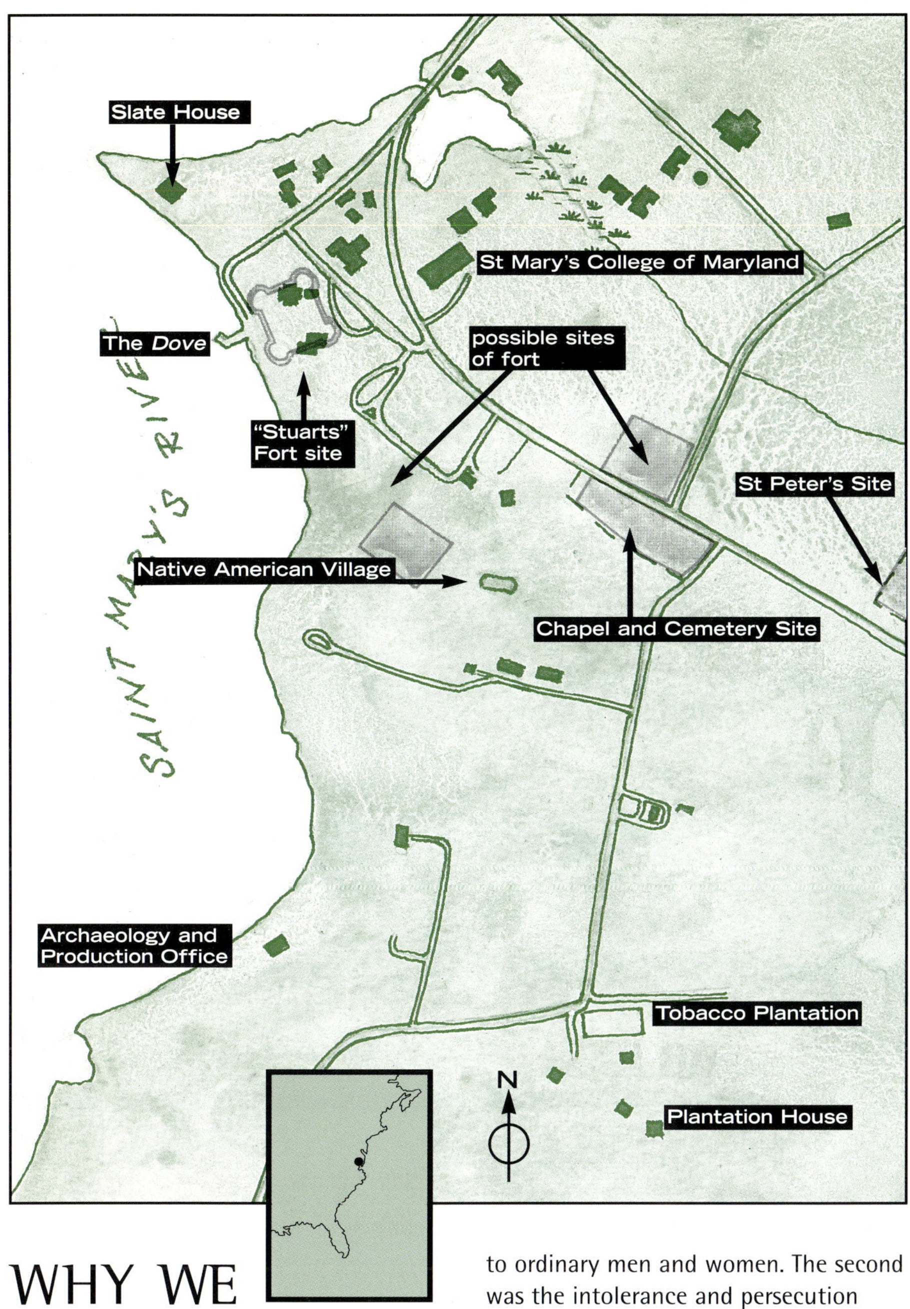

WHY WE WENT THERE

This would be TIME TEAM's first overseas site, and from the start, we were lucky in getting the full co-operation of Dr Henry Miller and his team at St Mary's City in Maryland, about 55 miles south-east of Washington DC. An outdoor museum had been created there, and buildings specially built in the early colonial style had become homes for a group of actors who had been trained to take on the roles of early settlers.

St Mary's was the result of three key cultural conditions of the 17th century. One was the relative lack of land in England available at a reasonable price to ordinary men and women. The second was the intolerance and persecution shown towards Roman Catholics in post-Reformation England. The third was the entrepreneurial desire to exploit the natural wealth of the newly found lands.

George Calvert, the 1st Baron Baltimore (?1579–1632), was English secretary of state until 1625, when he resigned after becoming a Catholic. Like many wealthy aristocrats, he was aware of the reports of the early journeys of Sir Walter Raleigh and others to the New World, which told of seas alive with fish, woods full of game, fields of fertile soil that produced abundant crops. In addition, once the perilous sea journey had been made, furs, land and other riches could be purchased relatively cheaply or even taken by force from the local population, which was in any case considered primitive.

Lord Baltimore was only too familiar with the tide of feeling against Catholics, which makes his conversion all the more extraordinary. Catholicism had been severely repressed during Elizabeth I's reign, and anti-Catholicism was further fuelled by the Spanish Armada of 1588 and the Gunpowder Plot of 1605. Lord Baltimore saw the new colony as a chance to create a society where Catholic beliefs and religious practices would be tolerated.

Roman Catholic monks before their martyrdom at Smithfield, London, in about 1600. *(Mary Evans Picture Library)*

He also wished to establish a society where investors could acquire not only land but also the status of having the title 'lord of the manor'. For all entrepreneurs hoping to found colonies, the key was to get together a group of wealthy investors who would fund the operation. Each investor would agree to pay for the passage of a number of colonists who, as indentured servants, would provide the labour force for the enterprise. In return for paying for the passage of five servants, which cost approximately £100, an investor was promised 2,000 acres of land. The colonist whose passage had been paid would, after working for his 'lord' for four years, be freed and given 50 acres of his own.

When the square-rigged sailing ships *Ark* and *Dove* sailed into Chesapeake Bay in 1634, they carried 140–160 colonists, who called themselves 'Adventurers'. The area where they landed is still relatively undeveloped today, and it is not hard to imagine their excitement and trepidation as they stepped ashore. Lord Baltimore was not among them – he had died two years earlier –

but his son Leonard became the first governor of the colony of Maryland, named after Charles I's queen, Henrietta Maria.

TIME TEAM had established with Dr Miller and his team a clear set of targets for the three days, each related to key elements of this early colony's history. After six years of research and excavation, local archaeologists had uncovered the area around the site of the brick chapel. This work included the excavation of a number of burials, some dating back to the period of early colonisation. We had been asked to see if we could use geophysics to locate the extent of the cemetery, which might turn out to be one of the largest undisturbed colonial graveyards.

In addition, we were to explore the site – 200 metres (650 ft) south-west of the chapel – of St Peter's , the mansion built between 1670 and 1680 as the home of the Chancellor Philip Calvert and later became the residence of the royal governors. This was a fascinating prospect as the mansion was one of the first to be built in colonial America and represented a very early planting of European culture in the New World. Blown up in 1694 in mysterious circumstances, it had been partially excavated in the 1930s, but its exact location was lost and no information survives to tell if the architectural evidence about the building is accurate.

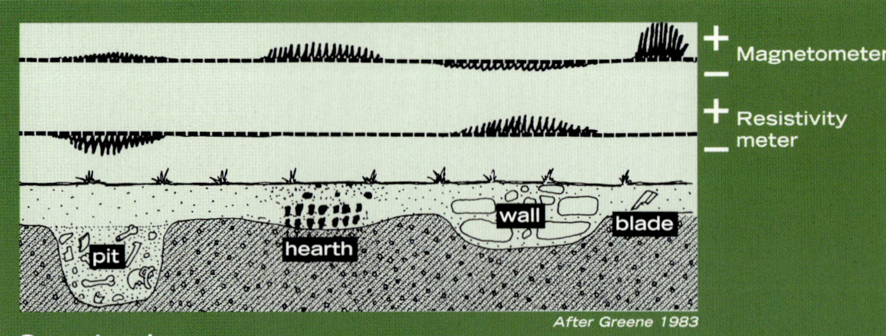

Geophysics

Geophysical surveying is used within known sites to suggest areas where excavation might be most profitable. Irregularities, or 'anomalies', indicating occupation debris or structures can be a very helpful guide in research work, in 'rescue archaeology' (when sites are shortly to be demolished by road building or other types of construction) and, indeed, in the context of our TIME TEAM weekends.

Two sorts of instruments are basically used. ***Resistivity meters*** detect the resistance of the subsoil to the passage of an electric current. This will pass easily through damp soil, but far less easily through dry compact material such as a buried wall or cobbled road. ***Magnetometers*** measure variations in the subsoil's magnetic characteristics. For instance, heating to 700°C (1290°F) or above, such as can occur in hearths, kilns and furnaces, causes the randomly aligned magnetic particles present in most soils to realign along the Earth's prevailing magnetic field; this new alignment will be retained even when the soil cools. In addition, solid features such as walls and road surfaces contain fewer magnetic minerals and so will produce lower readings than their surroundings.

Geophysics can be carried out quickly by using portable instruments that supply continuous readings. The results are displayed on a computer screen, usually in the form of linear graphs, with peaks and troughs indicating, say, points of high and low resistance.

Day One

As usual, the first goal was to see if geophysics could locate the structure of St Peter's, to provide us with a target for excavation. With the team recovering from jet-lag and the heat and humidity rising, progress was slow. We fairly quickly began to realise that excavation in this climate was going to be a long business, and the situation was not helped by the presence of 'chiggers' – mites that burrowed under the skin of the unsuspecting excavators.

Early records refer to colonists undergoing a 'seasoning', which included contracting a wide range of infections and fevers from which many died. Having arrived in late spring, it would not have been long before the settlers realised that the climate was not going to be as benign as they had hoped.

The St Peter's geophysics results

Native American smoking tobacco, from an engraving c.1600. *(Mary Evans Picture Library)*

and the rest of us!

With work underway at St Peter's, John Gater and Chris Gaffney began the arduous task of traversing the chapel site to see if they could determine to what extent the graves had been disturbed. The hope was that a natural boundary would exist between the disturbed area of graves and the undisturbed land around it, and that this would be traceable by geophysics. Fairly soon, however, it became clear that there was another level of recent archaeological disturbance in the form of numerous test pits. This was going to make the task much more difficult.

Stuart Ainsworth was keen to establish the main features of the St Mary's area and, in particular, to examine possible locations for the early fort. Forts were made of wood and were often built on sites that are subsequently redeveloped; therefore, finding the remains of this kind of feature can be a long shot. However, the importance of this building to the early inhabitants of the colony made it worth a try

With work underway, this gave Tony and other members of the team a chance to explore some of the 'living' exhibits, especially the display of early Native American culture. The first colonists were lucky in their initial contacts. The local Yaocomico tribe was friendly, as well as grateful for any assistance that the colonists could give them in their battles with the more aggressive Susquehannocks to the north. They showed the settlers how to make bread from maize and where the best supplies of game and other foods could

turned out to be highly successful. A clear square pattern of high resistance emerged, located within the wheat field that we had cut down. John Gater speculated that the strong signals could have been caused by the explosion and subsequent fire, which would first have wiped out the random magnetic field and subsequently allowed one with a uniform signal to become established.

Excavation began, and it was at this stage that we realised that there was going to be something of a clash of cultures between our normal ways of working and the ways of our American hosts. As the first spade of soil was excavated, it was immediately sieved, prior to the next shovelful being dug out. Although we had been told that the Americans sieve everything, it was only now that we understood the full implications of this method, which represented some fundamental differences between British and American archaeology. Relatively speaking, the Americans have less artefact evidence, and archaeological sites such as St Mary's are comparatively rarer than a typical British site; therefore, they treat their artefacts and sites with great reverence. Also, the majority of their finds come from the top layer of plough soil, so *all* the earth has to be carefully sieved. These facts conspire to mean that the process of excavation in the United States is, to British eyes, tortuously slow.

Gradually we negotiated some changes in the process to increase our speed. It was agreed that we could dig out a great deal of soil before any sieving had to begin – 'retrospective sieving' as one person put it – and the American diggers began to pick up the sense of urgency that was emanating from Phil

The Jesuits in St Mary's

The Roman Catholic Society of Jesus was founded by Ignatius Loyola in 1534. Its aims were educational work, the suppression of heresy, and missionary work among non-believers. During the 16th and 17th centuries, the members – priests known as Jesuits – achieved great success as missionaries in Japan, China and Paraguay and among Native Americans.

The Jesuits were one of the main investors in the settlement of St Mary's, no doubt attracted by the tolerant nature of the colony's founders towards Catholics, the opportunity to make a good profit and the chance to create a new mission for conversions in the New World. They paid for 20 of the initial settlers, and another 30 in the next decade. The Jesuit father, Andrew White, was among those who arrived in the *Ark*, and he kept a diary of both the journey and the early years of the colony. He noted the terror of the Native Americans when they saw the 300-ton ship, which they referred to as a 'canoe as big as an island'.

In the 1640s, the English Civil War arrived in Maryland and resulted in the deaths of several of the Jesuits, and in 1704, Catholicism was suppressed in the colony. However, before then, the priests had achieved some success in converting the indigenous population, and in 1667 they had built an impressive chapel, the first major brick building in St Mary's.

(Top) St Mary's City: Aerial view of the reconstruction of the settlers' village and the replica of the *Dove*. *(Mick Aston)*
(Above) Jesuits preaching to Native Americans in California, *c.* 1680. *(Mary Evans Picture Library)*

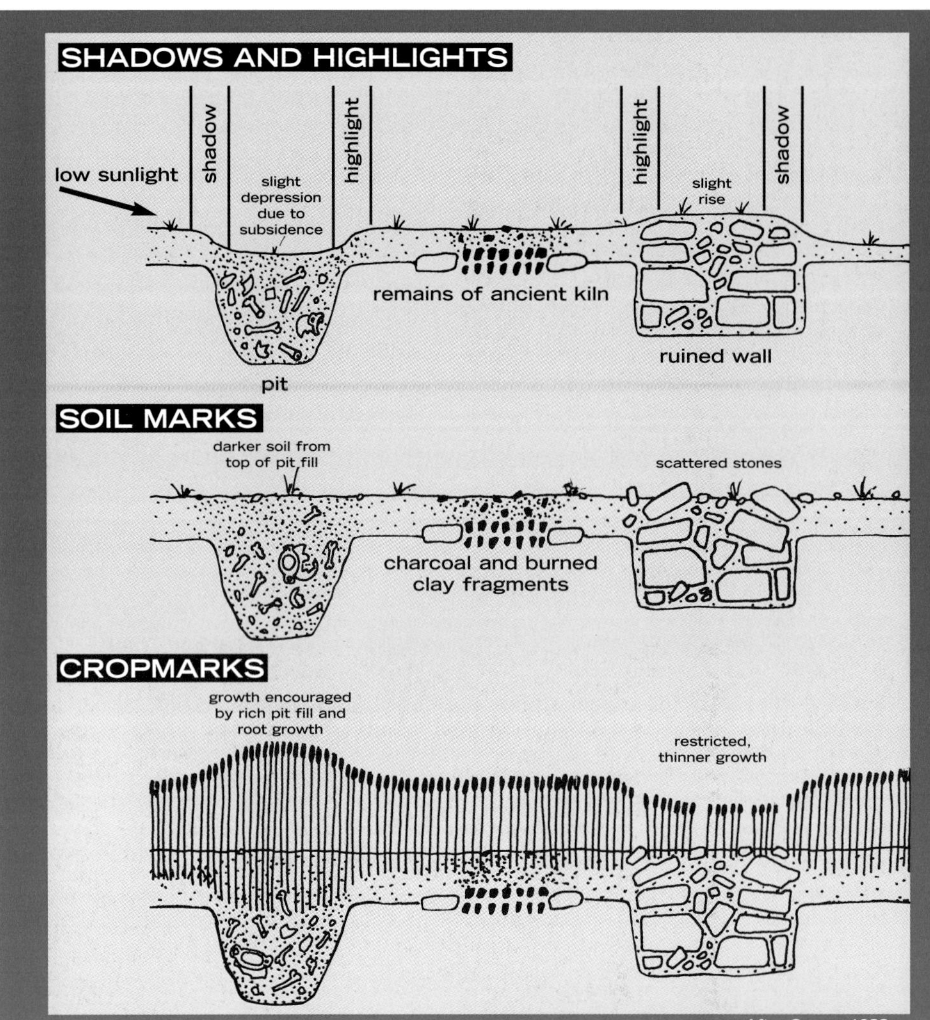

After Greene 1983

Marks on the landscape

What lies below the ground can leave clues on the surface. Depressions and raised soil can be detected on cleared ground when the sun is low on the horizon: the shadows and highlights will reveal patterns. The earth itself can contain soil marks – for instance, dark parts where ditches and pits have been filled in, bits of charcoal and clay where something was burned, and scattered stones where a wall or cobbled road once was. Finally, cropmarks – light and dark marks in growing crops, best seen in aerial photographs – are plants' reactions to the subsoil: they grow less and ripen first if they are deprived of water by hidden stone walls or packed stone layers, and will remain greener longer and be taller if they grow over a pit or ditch that has been infilled with soil.

be found, and the settlers were allowed to use the Yaocomico huts for shelter. In return, the indigenous population was given supplies of iron hoes, axes and trinkets. The small bells that today are often found on archaeological sites were particularly greatly valued.

The settlers also brought another highly prized metal – copper. Hitherto the Yaocomico had only been able to obtain this by trading far to the north and then it was supplied only in minute amounts. Now they received vast quantities in the form of copper kettles – the present-day equivalent would perhaps be teapots made of gold. These kettles were recycled and the metal used as jewellery and later as scrapers.

One other piece of information provided by the Indians was to have a critical effect on the colony's history: the ease with which tobacco could be cultivated in the hot, humid climate. Although Lord Baltimore had anticipated quick profits from the fur trade, his ultimate goal was for Maryland to have a mixed agricultural and industrial economy. However, tobacco soon began to dominate. It had a ready market in Europe and firmly established trading links. Soon everything was valued in tobacco. The Native Americans, who had introduced the use of clay pipes to the Europeans, began to make them in large numbers. We were later to see evidence of these pipes' popularity in the excavation in the graveyard: in the jawbone of one of the skeletons were a number of 'pipe facets', teeth worn down over time by the stem of a pipe.

At St Peter's, Phil had found his own

One of the skeletons found at St Mary's, its jawbone showing 'pipe facets', where the teeth have been worn down by pipe stems. *(Mick Aston)*

the south-east of the chapel site, which, Henry informed us, had some backing as a contender from local tradition. The geophysics produced a clear signal line, and Phil was brought in to dig an evaluation trench.

With temperatures climbing to 37.8°C (100°F), this was no mean task, but Phil and his American crew hacked into the soil and within two hours declared the site empty of finds and that the source of the signal was – geological! Stuart himself regarded the site near the inlet as too far from navigable access to be a possibility, and as this site had already had some work done on it, we resolved to explore the third, cropmark option the next day.

link with the original inhabitants – a beautiful projectile point (either a spear-head or an arrowhead) made from white quartz, which provided him with a fitting end to the first day.

Day Two

Excavations at the St Peter's site had progressed, and at last we had located traces of brick work. The bricks, made locally, are fairly distinctive and had turned up on other sites. We had also begun to find pieces of pottery imported from England, fragments of terracotta roof tiles and some fired shot. We knew that the cellar of the St Peter's mansion had been used as an armoury and that this had exploded in 1694. There was speculation that this had been a deliberate act, perpetrated by a governor keen to see Annapolis become the colony's capital (which it did the same year).

It was at this stage that Stuart and Carenza became interested in cropmarks that had been found on an early aerial photograph. These seemed to indicate a possible site for a fort. We already had two other options – one near the small inlet *(see map)* and another nearer to the chapel. Dr Miller was keen to resolve the dilemma, and Stuart was increasingly convinced that his site was the best bet.

In the graveyard, John and Chris, having completed their scan, reluctantly faced the fact that too much disturbance had occurred to allow an accurate idea of its extent. This freed them to chase the fort sites, and they first surveyed the area to

(Top) A trench at the St Peter's site, showing the excavation of one of the walls. *(Mick Aston)*
(Above) Inside a Native American hut reconstructed at St Mary's City. *(Mick Aston)*

Day Three

A full-scale replica of the 50 ton *Dove* set sail in the morning with members of the TIME TEAM on board. The wonderful sight of this beautiful vessel approaching the tree-lined coast made those of us still on land experience the kind of awe that must have been felt in 1634 by the Native Americans, who believed the ship to have been made from a single massive tree.

In the graveyard, the excavation of one of the bodies had been completed. Later research would show that the skeleton, with its multiple pipe facets, was male. By now, an expert on skeletons – Doug Owsley, from the Smithsonian Institution in Washington DC – had joined us. One fascinating aspect of his research has been his experimental work on the relative proportions of carbon 12 and carbon 13 in skeletons. As we eat, we incorporate carbon into our bones. It has been discovered that people brought up on a diet predominantly consisting of wheat, barley and rye have a larger amount of carbon 12 than those brought up on maize, which produces a predominance of carbon 13. Doug's work suggests that these differences might show which skeletons in the graveyard belonged to early European settlers and which to people born in St Mary's and raised on the maize diet found there.

St Peter's had now produced both a front and rear wall with differing 'bonds' – the term used to describe the way bricks are laid. The rear was in English bond and the front in the more attractive Flemish bond. Carenza had also begun to notice features on the aerial photographs that indicated possible formal gardens.

Stuart and Dr Miller had discussed the possibility that the evidence for the third fort site actually comprised lines created by grandstands built for a celebration in 1934. Tim O'Riordan, the archaeologist in charge of excavations at St Mary's, also pointed out that few surface finds – which might have indicated an early fort – had been located in this area. Yet Stuart was still convinced that this was the site. Although John and Chris were unable to find any clear geophysics targets indicating a fort wall, they did find an area of high resistance in the middle of their survey area. With only a few hours remaining, we decided to dig an evaluation trench. Almost immediately, Phil – now suffering from the effects of dehydration – located brick work. As more brick emerged, it became clear that we had found the chimney stack of a hitherto undiscovered colonial house. Pieces of English pottery also came to light, and this meant that we ended our weekend having made a real discovery that delighted Dr Miller and his team.

In just three days, we had found the foundations of St Peter's – one of the most important buildings in early colonial America – and had located what appeared to be an important merchant's house. Stuart had also contributed to the on-going fort search, which only time and excavation by the American archaeologists will resolve.

Final thoughts from Mick

I had never been to the US before, so I was very interested to see how American archaeologists worked and what sorts of sites they had. I was particularly pleased that we were dealing with a colonial site where some of our English ancestors had lived.

Everyone at St Mary's City was very friendly and helpful, though all thought the progress was slow. Still, the end results were spectacular and very useful to Henry Miller and his team. I particularly enjoyed steering the replica ship, the Dove, *under full sail for over an hour on the river!*

(Top left) The replica of the 50-ton *Dove*, which was used by the first colonists primarily to carry baggage and other goods. *(Mick Aston)*
(Top right) Reconstructed settlers' buildings at St Mary's City. Did the rediscovered colonial house resemble one of these? *(Mick Aston)*
(Above) Computer reconstruction of the settlers' fort, sited where Stewart Ainsworth expects it to be found.

BIRMINGHAM

WEST MIDLANDS

WHAT MIGHT HAVE HAPPENED

Matthew Boulton felt a sense of great satisfaction as he walked from the Principal Building to the new mint operation. The cogs and shafts rumbled, the coins in their thousands slid from the presses and he knew that the first steam-powered mint in the world was a success. From the early days of experiment on the first Boulton & Watt engine to this hive of activity was a mere ten years, and yet so much had been achieved. Boulton & Watt engines were operating throughout the country, and Boulton's Manufactory was creating products ranging from the utilitarian to highly crafted clocks and cases – art and industry truly combined. As Boulton looked back to his Manufactory, and another group of European visitors arrived to view the wonders of the Soho works, his mind turned to new overseas markets for his coins, but then his thoughts shifted to his greatest desire – to produce the national penny and halfpenny.

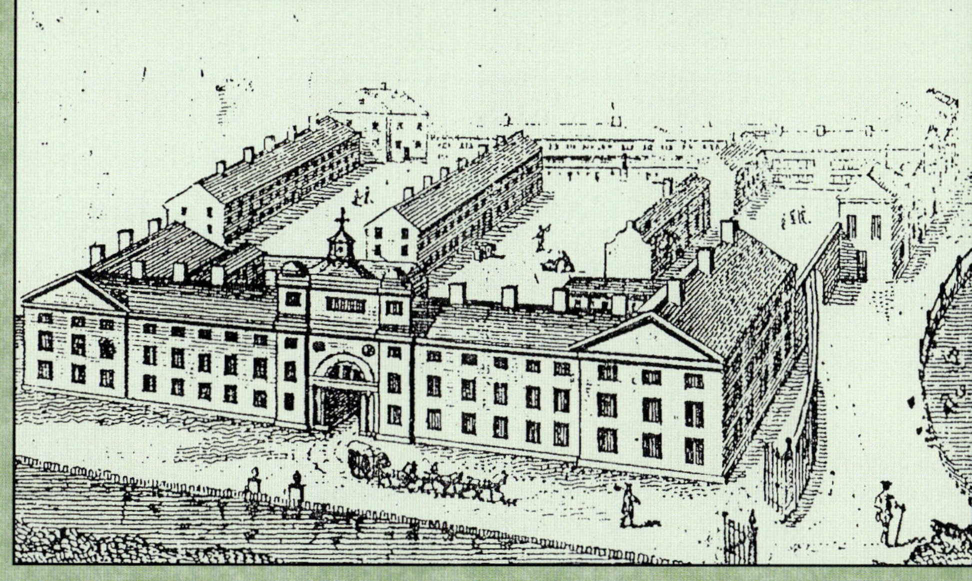

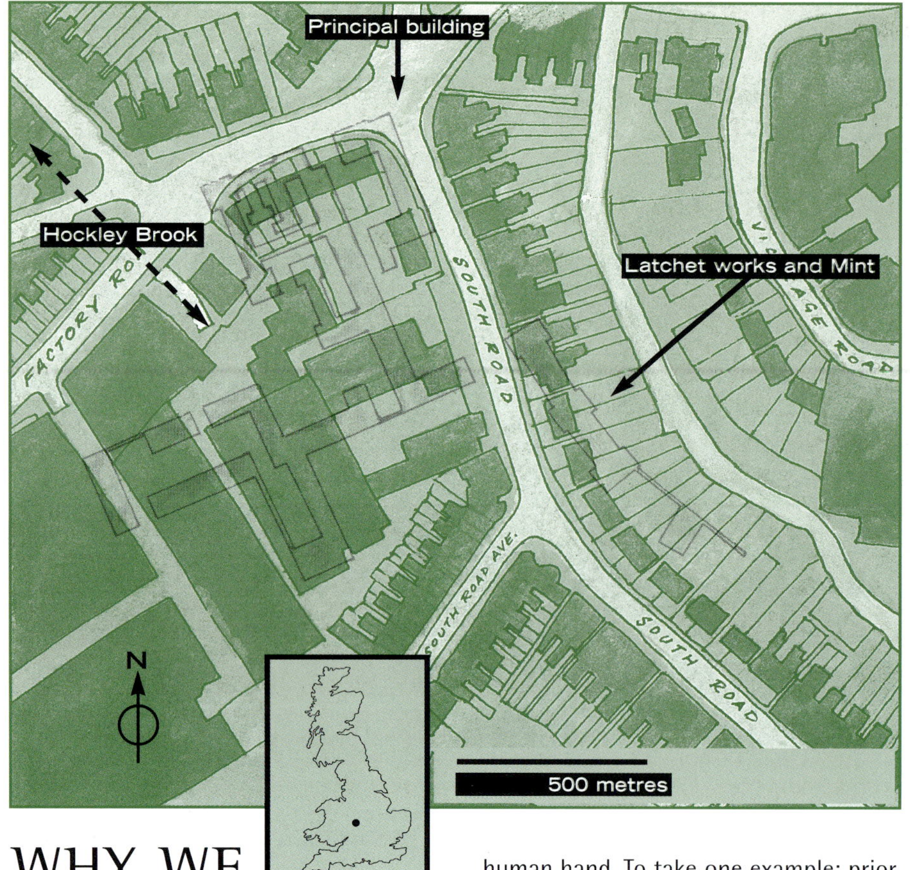

WHY WE WENT THERE

This site represented two firsts for TIME TEAM. It was the first time we had excavated an industrial archaeology site and it was our first inner-city back garden location!

Industrial archaeology presents some unusual challenges for archaeologists. It is usually associated with sites in existence only since the 17th century or later, although earlier industrial sites can be included. Many of the sites that have been excavated are those associated with the start of the Industrial Revolution, the classic case being those in the Ironbridge Gorge in Shropshire, where in the early 1700s Abraham Darby produced iron using coal-fired furnaces, and where the world's first cast-iron bridge was erected in 1779. Archaeologists search for factories and workshops and the remains of the machines that were once contained within them.

This period also marked a massive increase in artefacts and the beginning of machine production, which makes it harder to attribute objects to a particular human hand. To take one example: prior to the 18th century, coins were generally made by hand-powered presses, which could turn out – at most – 50 to 60 coins an hour. With the invention of the steam-driven mint, that rate increased to tens of thousands, and the objects produced had a regularity and consistency that had not been seen before. For instance, Samuel Colt's new gun-machining factory in Hartford, Connecticut produced parts so accurately that they could easily be exchanged between different firearms of the same type.

This was the beginning of the end of a world in which objects were made on a 'bespoke' basis. Mass production was on its way, and it resulted in a level of manufacture that could no longer be measured in human terms. The power of human and animal muscle was replaced, first, by water mills that produced flour, cloth and processed metal, and then – and most importantly – by steam engines fed by a seemingly inexhaustible supply of coal. Across the world, new industrial centres developed next to large coal fields – at Pittsburgh, Pennsylvania, along the Rhine in Germany, at Liège in Belgium – and the remains of the first and perhaps the most important of these are now located under the backstreets of Handsworth in Birmingham, where we found ourselves on the first day of this TIME TEAM.

In 1761, next to the Hockley Brook, Matthew Boulton (1728–1809) set up a small water-powered factory that he called the Soho Manufactory. When engineer and inventor James Watt arrived in 1774, the two worked on an advanced form of steam engine that would crank the Industrial Revolution into full motion. Thanks to research by local archaeologists – in particular, George Demidowicz and Nick Molyneux – into the historical records related to this period, we knew what the Boulton Manufactory once looked like. However, although this site had been important enough to have a good number of plans, drawings and engravings associated with it, there were still many gaps in the records. In addition, like many such sites, it had since been intensively redeveloped. One of our main challenges for the weekend was to see if we could locate it below the ground. Most of the Manufactory was inaccessible because of building, but the situation was different for the mint that Boulton had set up in 1788.

We were faced by a set of neat, semi-detached houses with gardens on which some of their owners had clearly lavished a lot of care and attention. Somewhere under this lot was one of the world's most important sites of industrial archaeology. Our local punter Dylan Close, who was going to help us

Matthew Boulton, founder of the Soho Manufactory in 1761. *(Mary Evans Picture Library)*

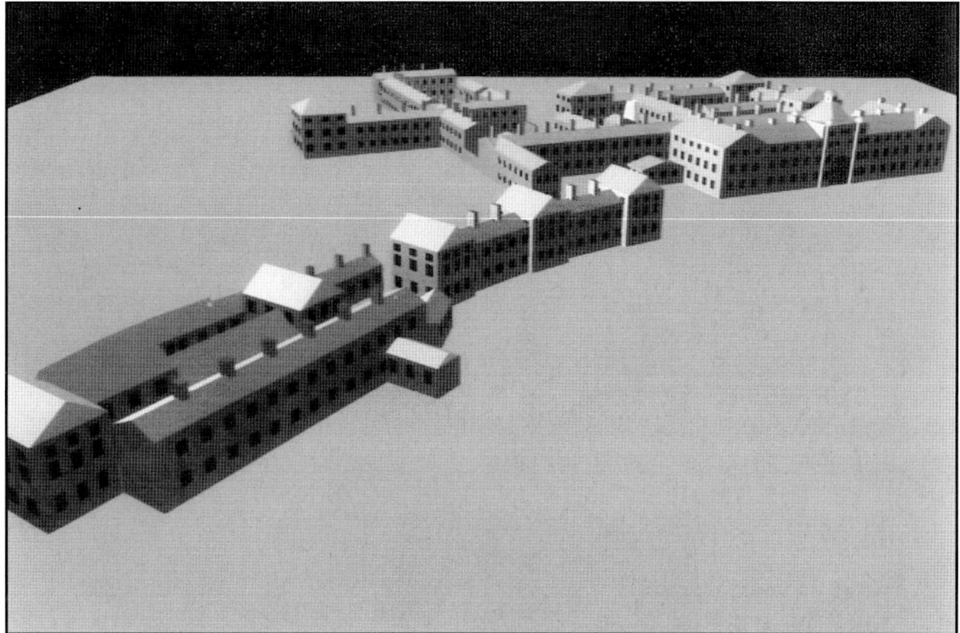

liaise with the home owners, had already begun the tricky business of gaining access. His own parents' house lay in the middle of the area we were interested in, and he assured us that they would be perfectly happy to have bits of their garden dug up. Dylan was the key to our strategy. From George's plans, we had an idea of where the mint lay, but could Dylan get us into his neighbours' back gardens and would we be allowed to dig holes in them?

Day One

To point us in the right direction, we had some initial evidence from a small trench that had been dug in a back garden two months previously and which we now began re-excavating. The main idea was that, if we could locate some of the key features in the ground at certain accessible points, we would be able to relate these exactly to one of archaeologist George Demidowicz's mint plans and this would lead us to other elements in the puzzle. Although all that had appeared in this garden hole (Trench 1) was the base of a brick-lined tunnel, this was important. First, it told us that parts of the factory had survived intact (George was able to identify the bricks as from the Boulton Soho period), and second, the tunnel was part of a network that might lead to other locations.

An 18th- and early 19th-century steam-powered factory was based on one or more large engines that required a massive investment of labour and money to construct. From these engines would run a number of rotating shafts that supplied power, via pulley wheels and leather belts, to other machines. At Boulton's mint in 1826, one steam engine drove four coin presses, and the engine was also linked by shafts running through brick tunnels to six presses that cut out coin blanks in another building. By locating one of these tunnels, we hoped to follow it to the 'cutting-out' room and then trace it back to the main steam engine.

George was also able to supply another bit of crucial information, his detective work illustrating a fascinating aspect of industrial archaeology. In 1850, a sale had been held of the mint's steam engine and all its working parts. In the sale particulars were detailed measurements of the shafts driven by the steam engine; together they measured about 62 m (203 ft), running in a single length. This meant that, if we could find a recognisable part of the tunnel, we could measure from it to the likely location of the side tunnel to the steam engine in the mint – and then dig! In the opposite direction, the tunnel was thought to lead into the 'cutting-out' room. This was in a separate building that had once been called the Latchet Works (a 'latchet' was a particular kind of buckle); in 1825, this had been converted to become part of the mint.

On this first morning, our measuring

involved a lot of clambering over hedges and passing of tapes over fences, but it eventually led us to the back garden of Mr and Mrs Close, Dylan's parents. In fact, the 'cutting-out' room appeared to be under their patio! After assurances from Dylan, Phil set to with a pickaxe to remove slabs and patio foundations. Throughout the entire weekend, Dylan and George's enthusiasm was to drive us along. It was clear that a patio would not stand in their way.

As well as the tunnel for the shaft, we hoped to discover the foundation wall of the 'Principal Building' of the main Manufactory complex, which might be

(Top left) Aerial view over the back gardens of Handsworth, Birmingham, under which lie the remains of Boulton's Manufactory. *(Mick Aston)*
(Top right) Computer reconstruction of Boulton's Manufactory.
(Above) The brick-lined tunnel in Trench 1. *(Mick Aston)*

Radar

Radar emits waves of electromagnetic radiation. As these strike the boundary between two different materials, or between a material and a void, they are bounced back to a receiver. The radar apparatus measures the length of time that the signal takes to return, and these measurements can be converted into distances. The initial images produced are vertical slices through the site, representing the various times it has taken the signal to return. A number of these vertical slices, carried out at close intervals, can be converted into a horizontal plan.

In general, we have found radar difficult to interpret, and it has certainly not become the answer to an archaeologist's prayer, as was predicted in the 1980s. By and large, it seems to need large voids or very clear, simple targets to produce usable data. We are generally sceptical of the results it achieves.

100 m (328 ft) away under the forecourt of a factory opposite Dylan's house. If we could find the corner of the grand classical front of this building – which had been designed by architect James Wyatt to look like a great country mansion – we would know where all of the other buildings lay below the ground but which were now mostly inaccessible.

The company occupying the site gave us permission to excavate the forecourt. Still, as with many industrial sites, such later development meant that, at the end of Day One, we were facing a daunting combination of concrete, tarmac and gravel that would require a JCB to penetrate. There was also a strong smell of petrol.

Day Two

With Phil persevering on the patio site, and the shaft area also being excavated, it was time for Robin to delve into the archives with Nick Molyneux. Matthew Boulton had lived during one of the most exciting periods in the development of science and technology. New inventions abounded, and for Boulton, it was natural that his scientific work would be accompanied by an interest in the arts and philosophy. He was a member of the Lunar Society, whose participants – Erasmus Darwin (Charles's grandfather), Joseph Priestley, James Watt and Josiah Wedgwood, among others – met monthly when the moon was full (hence the society's name) to share the excitement of their discoveries. Boulton was also a scrupulous record-keeper, and luckily many of his business records containing details of his beloved Manufactory still survive. George had been able to use them to reconstruct a bird's-eye view of all the buildings. Now excitement similar to that of the Lunar Society meetings accompanied our efforts to rediscover the Soho works.

Boulton first came to the Handsworth site in 1761 and purchased a 'poor and weak' water mill, which was kept in operation until the 1850s. His first use of steam power was with a pump to recycle water to the head race channel that supplied the waterwheel. The Manufactory initially made buttons, buckles and small decorative metal-work called 'toys'. However, when Boulton's entrepreneurial skills met Watt's inventive genius in 1774, a revolution began.

BOX: *(Left)* Using ground radar on a patio in one of the Handsworth gardens. *(Right)* Printout of the radar results, showing the vertical slices through the site. *(Mick Aston)*
(Above) Eighteenth-century workshop at the Soho works, where steam engines are being constructed. *(Mary Evans Picture Library)*

Watt's improvements to the steam engine – primarily the condenser, which allowed steam to condense outside the main cylinder – increased its power and efficiency. By 1800, most industrial areas of the country had Boulton & Watt engines operating, but many of the early ones were used to pump water out of the tin mines of Cornwall. Steam engines also required a good supply of water, and this was provided by means of deep wells. At Soho, water was taken from a nearby artificial channel and brought to a well, and our next target was find this. Although the mint and steam engine house had been destroyed, the deep well shaft should still be there.

Due to the dense cover of concrete and tarmac over a lot of the site, we had brought in a radar team to locate possible locations for excavation. Radar is reckoned to be best for finding voids (empty spaces), and with luck, a well for a steam engine might be discovered. Venturing into yet another garden, the radar scanners searched for evidence.

By using the data from the radar plotting and some of George's detailed plans, we got an approximate fix for the likely location of the steam engine. From the plans, we knew that the centre of the main shaft tunnel was 2.1 m (7 ft) away from the outside wall of the engine house, and that approximately 2.4 m (8 ft) further in lay the steam engine. Our excavations in Trench 2, in the next garden to Trench 1, had located a junction in the main shaft, so we measured 4.6 m (15 ft) in from this point.

The shaft junction in Trench 2, with the base of the pulley supports (directly in front of the tree). *(Mick Aston)*

To get an idea of the kind of machine we were looking for, we took a trip to the Birmingham Museum of Science and Industry and viewed one of the few surviving examples in action. Boulton and Watt had sold construction plans for these machines and their key parts to factories all over the country and later throughout the world. Many are over 9 metres (30 ft) in height, and the main beam can weigh several tons. Each also needed to be supplied with thousands of gallons of water, to produce the steam, and all this required masses of piping and other structures. After examining one of the engines, it was evident why such substantial buildings were needed to house them.

By the end of Day Two, the factory dig had begun to face serious problems. The source of the petrol smell had been traced to a large fuel tank that required the attention of experts from the local fire brigade. The depth of the excavation and the considerable amount of debris meant that shoring was vital.

In Trench 3, inches under the Closes' patio, Phil had located part of a wall foundation constructed of bricks that George confirmed as being the kind used by Boulton elsewhere at Soho. Button blanks – pieces of bone with holes cut out by a stamping machine – had also been found. In Trench 1, which we had re-excavated, more of the tunnel had been discovered. Even more of it was found in Trench 2 next door, as well as the junction that may have carried the main pulley wheel drive from the steam engine. If this proved to be the case, we would have the clearest pointer yet for the location of the steam engine.

Day Three

By now, we had uncovered more of the shaft tunnel in Trenches 1 and 2 and had found the base for the pulley supports at the junction. There was now the possibility that, by excavating about

midway between the wall footings under Dylan's parents' patio and the tunnel in Trenches 1 and 2, we might find the end wall of the former Latchet Works (which, from 1825, became part of the mint) in yet another garden of another house. This dig – Trench 5 – fairly quickly revealed more of the tunnel, a major brick wall beneath it, copper coin blanks and pipe stems - the archaeological equivalent of today's cigarette butts. Although the end wall was not found, the area of the wall within the Latchet Works was identified and so the position of the whole building could be fixed beneath these Handsworth houses and gardens.

The 'Principal Building' trench (Trench 4) was now of vast dimensions, with mains gas and another fuel tank making an appearance. The presence of these prevented us from going any further, but the deep, soft fill behind the wall – which also had a white-washed interior – indicated that this was probably the front wall of the main building, and that the cellar floor was still below but too deep to be excavated. The wall foundation in Phil's trench under the patio was hard to locate on its own, but from the walls found in Trench 5, it was clear that we had successfully uncovered a small part of the front wall of the 'cutting-out' room. The centre of this room was now under Dylan's parents living room!

Nick had unearthed some plans of the Bombay mint erected in the early 1820s, shortly before the reorganisation of the Soho mint. Using these plans, we could at least imagine the kind of structure that we had discovered under the back gardens – particularly the 'cutting-out' room with its classical columns.

Boulton's Manufactory sent goods throughout the world. Not only humble buttons and buckles were made here, but also, as the factory flourished, high-status objects - sophisticated lamps and gilded clocks, one of which found its way to the royal court of Catherine the Great in Russia. After his death in 1809, Boulton was succeeded by his son, and the site continued in production until the early 1860s, when most of it was torn down. For a short time, only the Principal Building was left standing, but it was finally demolished in 1863.

By finding the main mint building, two parts of the Latchet Works, the front wall of the Principal Building and the steam engine well, we had been able to locate the information contained in George's drawings and plans exactly on the ground. This should protect the Manufactory's remains should any redevelopment of the area be contemplated, and should also enable local archaeologists to unearth more of the factory at a future date.

Coins and conscience

Boulton was a great enthusiast for minting coins. He employed skilled engravers to create magnificent portraits to adorn them, and he also introduced the 'cartwheel' coin, which had the benefit of being worth its weight in metal. At a time of counter-feiting and devaluation, such a coin had a secure value.

Boulton's social conscience also extended to developing the first workers' insurance scheme and to building housing for his employees. He was certainly a man that all of the TIME TEAM would have liked to have met.

Final thoughts from Mick

I find it difficult to believe that we actually made a programme in Birmingham, near where I come from, in such apparently inhospitable archaeological circumstances. But the end results were stupendous: Boulton's Manufactory – for its time and of its type, one of the most important archaeological sites in the world.

My best memories, however, are of the 1779 working steam engine in Birmingham's industrial museum, at each stroke lifting a ton of water. The smoke, steam, noise and smells all brought the Industrial Revolution to life.

(Above) Phil and the petrol tank in the 'Principal Building' trench in the factory forecourt. *(Mick Aston)*
BOX: Some of the copper coin blanks found in Trench 5. *(Mick Aston)*

LAUNCESTON

CORNWALL

WHAT MIGHT HAVE HAPPENED

The woman knew that she was dying. As if the dreaded disease were not bad enough, she was now suffering from blinding headaches. This was a punishment from God – at least that was what many of her fellow sufferers believed. She dreaded the long walk to the edge of the town to beg for alms, which she knew she would have to undertake the following day. The old man who had just arrived in the colony had promised her something to relieve her symptoms. A letting of blood would be needed, followed by a poultice of yarrow, but the thought of it all filled her with fear.

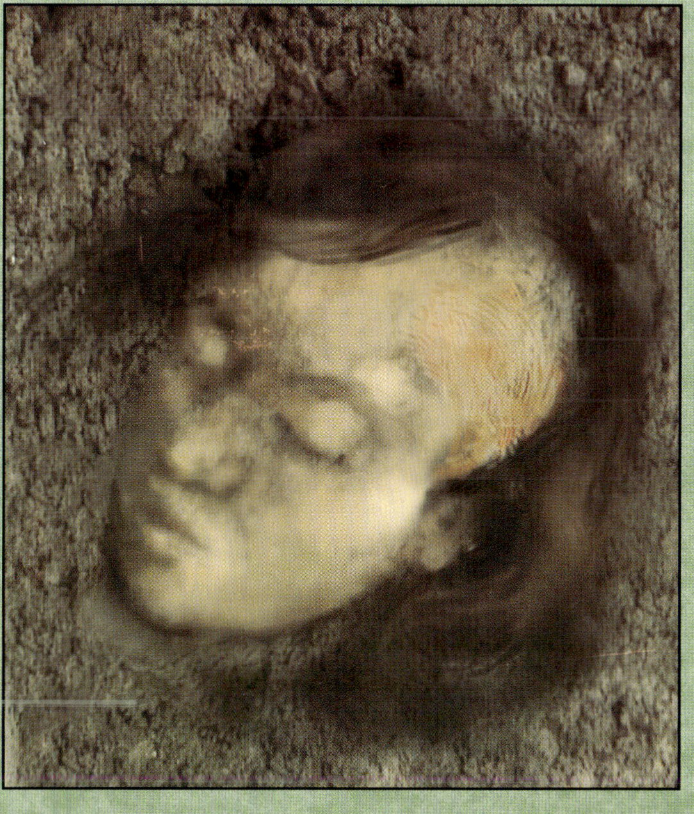

Computer reconstruction of the head of the young woman whose skeleton was found at Launceston.

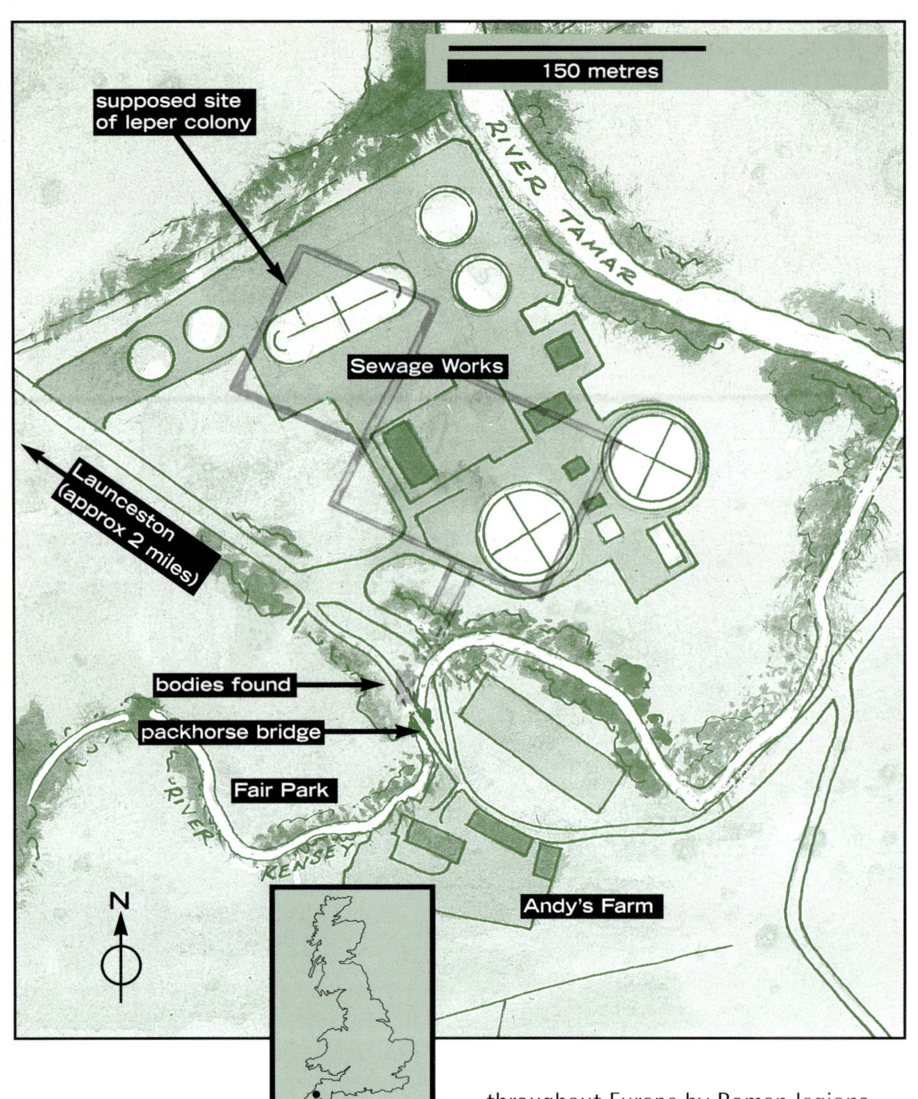

WHY WE WENT THERE

This TIME TEAM venture began with a letter from a viewer. Andy Reeve, who runs a riding centre near Launceston in Cornwall, had a problem. While exploring for a burst water pipe, he had unearthed the remains of a number of skeletons. There had been no obvious finds among the bones that could aid in their identification, but Andy was intrigued by the fact that local maps identified the fields near his farm as the 'Lazar Grounds' and thus a likely site of a medieval leper colony.

Leprosy was once a widespread disease and, in one form, highly infectious; it is spread by droplet infection from the nose or mouth. It was once believed that it had been brought into Britain by knights returning from the Crusades, but it is more likely that it was spread throughout Europe by Roman legions and, over the years, gradually took hold. Leper colonies known as 'lazar houses' or 'lazar grounds' – after St Lazarus, patron saint of lepers – were created outside many major towns, often set up by wealthy noblemen anxious to do good deeds. At the height of the disease, more than 200 such colonies had been established in England, 27 in Cornwall alone.

The early lazar houses were often chapel-like buildings, with half the structure set aside for worship and half for the care of the sick. Because of their segregation from the towns, these communities were often self-sufficient in food; the members also cared for their ill brethren themselves, and they had permission to bury their own dead. The progress of the disease can be so horrific – the face becomes disfigured, fingers, toes and limbs are lost and the cartilage and bone in the nose erodes – that it created great fear and prejudice, and this ensured an enforced isolation of the lazar houses. In Launceston in the late Middle Ages, it was believed that leprosy could even be contracted by touching the stones of the hospital building.

The leprosy epidemic peaked in Europe in about 1300, and a century later, the disease had almost disappeared, except in Scandinavia. Today, while it continues to affect approximately 20 million people worldwide, its infectiousness has greatly reduced. Only 3 per cent of the human population is susceptible to this disease, and of those, only people living in prolonged close contact with an infected person risk contracting it.

Andy Reeve, obviously keen to find out more about his bones, had invited us down. With the help of Nick Johnson and the Cornwall Archaeological Unit, we began work on a wet and windy day

(Top) A 13th-century French leper house. The figure in the middle is begging alms and shaking a rattler to warn people of his approach. *(Mary Evans Picture Library)*
(Above) Doctors discuss a patient in the early stages of leprosy, from Dickmut's *Regimen sanitatis* of 1482. *(Mary Evans Picture Library)*

in spring with Phil suffering from an infection of his own – flu – which manifested itself in a variety of unpleasant ways!

Day One

One of our first tasks was to find out if there was anything else that could explain the presence of the skeletons. For example, there had been a Civil War battle near the site, during which a large number of dead had been buried locally. Robin was keen to do some research in the excellent small museum and historic library that is hidden in one of Launceston's back streets.

For those who have never visited Launceston, it is worth mentioning what an historically important and attractive town it is. The former capital of Cornwall, it has an imposing castle, first built by Robert of Mortain, half-brother of William the Conqueror, but what remains probably dates from the 12th and 13th centuries. St Mary Magdalene's Church, with its 14th-century tower ordered by the Black Prince, was largely rebuilt in the 16th century by Sir Henry Trecarrel, and its outer walls, decorated in a highly elaborate style, are a monument to the stonemason's art. On the south wall is a granite figure of a saint lying face down. According to the pamphlet, *A Series of Parish Walks in North Cornwall*, published by Cornwall County Council, children of the town used to believe that a stone thrown up and lodged on the saint's back would bring good luck. They would sing this rhyme:

Mary, Mary Magdalene,
Under a stony tree.
I throw a pebble on your back.
What will you send to me?

It is very likely that many of Cornwall's greatest nobles would have set out for the Crusades from this church. There is some evidence that the leper colony was specifically set up as expiation for what was thought to have been the Crusaders' introduction of leprosy into Cornwall.

Robin located a 17th-century document in the possession of the Town Council of Dunheved (the original name of Launceston), which describes the 13th-century boundaries of the colony. This document contains an extract from a pre-1258 charter written by Robert Fissacre and witnessed by Richard, Earl of Cornwall (1227–72), who was the son of King John. The key text read:

To the lepers of Gillemartin at Lanceueton in pure and perpetual alms, for an exchange which they made with us of their tenement which they had in Lanceueton ... to have and to hold to them and their successors freely, quietly, peaceably and wholly ... I have given and confirmed ... as the boundaries there wind, to wit, as the water Kensi [Kensey] descends into the River Tambie [Tamar] and so ascending by the water of the Kensi even to the ditch of Wittemore, and near that ditch as far as the well which is at the head of the causeway, so that they may have that rivulet of that well for their offices; and along near the causeway even to the wall of the cemetery of the aforesaid chapel and thence towards the north as far as the land of the Park ... and thence over Meddelonde as the boundary winds above Holemede; and from Holemede as far as the rivulet of Colevorde lake ... and thence descending along the Tamar even to the Kensi ...

The text also refers to land and a chapel that existed on that land.

In what proved to be a fascinating exercise, we compared the boundaries outlined in the charter with modern Ordnance Survey maps, and then attempted to locate them on the ground. Clearly some of the features mentioned in the charter have survived – the rivers, for instance – but there also appeared to be definite signs of former boundaries where the hedges had been grubbed out. It was an exciting moment when we realised that traces of these ancient boundaries still existed, particularly because of the archaeological importance of putting a definable perimeter around the colony.

While this research was going on, Phil had proceeded to sort out the skeletal remains that Andy Reeve had discovered. In the wet and the mud, this proved a testing task. Unfortunately, when Andy had randomly dug his trench to locate the pipe, he had smashed across the bones, so the first job was to clear up the mess and to try to see if any of the skeletons remained intact and articulated – that is, with the bones still attached at the joints.

The way in which a body has been buried can give important clues to its origins. If it has been laid out flat with

(Top) Computer reconstruction of Launceston leper colony.
(Above) A Crusader portrayed as a Christian hero, from a popular 19th-century Spanish print. *(Mary Evans Picture Library)*

that the lack of clear linear features might indicate something else.

With the permission of a local farmer, we sank our first trench to see what might be causing the field's lumpy appearance and the high resistance. By mid-afternoon, the trench, which had been extended up to the hedge-line surrounding Andy's skeleton trench, had revealed nothing that was man-made. Near the boundary edge, we found no artefacts, and the area of high resistance proved to be geological. In this part of Cornwall, there are plentiful strata of wolframite, an ore used in hardening metal. This was present throughout the field and had created the signals picked up by the geophysics team.

The lack of any finds led us to rethink our strategy. Perhaps we were on the wrong side of the road?

We already knew that, when the huge sewage works that dominated the other side of the road had been built in 1880-1907, the local builders had found a fragment of a wall. Could a leprosy hospital have been located here? With the permission of South West Water, excavation of this area had already begun under Carenza's direction, and by the end of Day One, we had started to see signs of building stone.

Day Two

Unfortunately, the trench in the sewage works proved unhelpful – the wall remains were relatively modern. We decided to extend the geophysics survey

hands crossed on the chest and the body orientated towards the east, this indicates a Christian burial. If it is disarticulated and buried with no orientation or signs of any care taken in the laying-out, this suggests a pit into which bodies have been thrown after a battle. Although we could get some information from these more obvious signs, Margaret Cox, our expert from Bournemouth University who would be joining us the next day, would be able to glean a great deal more from her analysis of the bones, especially if we could find enough in reasonable condition. By lunchtime, Phil had cleared away the debris and located a possible grave-cut – a line in the earth that, in cross-section, shows a difference between the natural soil and the infill of a grave – and a human skull. Skulls are important because they can tell us much more about the dead than some of the other parts of the body. Sex, age and diet, among other things, can all be determined from a well-preserved skull.

If the bodies Andy had found were associated with a leprosy hospital, it was likely that there would be an adjacent building or even the chapel itself. John and his team had started a geophysics survey of the most likely location for this – a field covered in lumps and bumps. This immediately began to show up areas of high resistance, some of which might be walls or other parts of a building. John, however, was concerned

(Top left) Part of the excavations at Launceston. *(Mick Aston)*
(Top right) Phil digging in the trench where Andy found the skeleton. The skull has been uncovered, and the crossing of the arms over the chest is just apparent. *(Mick Aston)* *(Above)* The fully uncovered skeleton. *(Mick Aston)*

towards Launceston on the off-chance that the buildings may have been located further north. Mick and Nick Johnson also felt that a trench inside the enclosure with the skeletons might answer the question: was this a small graveyard standing alone? According to Mick, there are several small sites in Cornwall and the West Country where a few graves were located within a tiny enclosure with its own chapel.

With Phil's cold getting no better, we were lucky to have on hand a group of medieval reconstruction experts – The White Company – to mix some potions. We wanted to know how our lepers might have been cared for and just what some of their symptoms would have been. Among the herbs that were growing all around Andy's farm was yarrow (*Achillea millefolium*), which in the Middle Ages was used in a well-known balm for leprosy. Feverfew (*Tanacetum parthenium*) would have been employed as a fever-reducer (as its name implies).

Because of the numbness of the extremities, a classic symptom of the disease, sufferers were unaware that they were constantly injuring their hands and feet; these injuries would lead to secondary infection, gangrene and the loss of fingers, toes and sometimes whole limbs. The disease also caused the reabsorption of calcium in bone, including the bony structures of the nose and mouth. This led to the destruction of the nose, palate and gums, and as well as the terrible disfigurement this caused, it meant that the lepers found it impossible to eat anything but the softest food.

Phil's condition was not improved by Margaret Cox's insistence that he climb into a complete protective body suit before lifting out the now virtually complete skeleton. Because we hoped to do a DNA analysis of the body, we had to be careful to allow as little contamination from modern debris as possible. Mind you, considering how much Phil was sneezing, this seemed a forlorn hope.

DNA, a two-stranded molecule in the nucleus of every cell, contains, in chemically coded form, all the information needed to build, control and maintain living organisms, including human bodies, bacteria and other tiny structures. Tiny amounts can, with difficulty, be extracted from ancient bones and teeth, and analysed to reveal specific details about diseases. For instance, a sample can be tested for the presence of antibodies specific to leprosy. However, our worries about the contamination of the graveyard bones later proved to be justified: it made it impossible to do an accurate DNA analysis and so this information was lost to us.

However, in the meantime, Margaret was able to tell us some fascinating details about our skeleton. First, it had once been a girl or young woman. The fact that her hands were turned in – clenched across the chest – indicated a Christian burial, and clenched hands are known to be associated with some types of leprosy. Only after we had completed

(Top left) Aerial view of the Launceston sewage works. *(South West Water)*
(Top right) The excavations at the sewage works. The medieval stonework is coming into view. *(Mick Aston)*
(Above) Phil dressed in the protective body suit, prior to removing the skeleton from the trench. *(Mick Aston)*

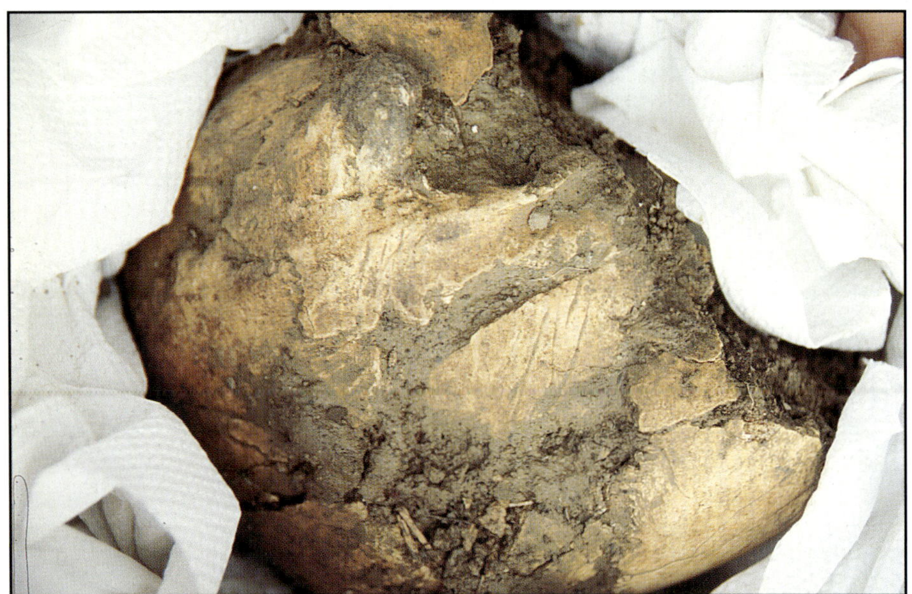

the painstaking job of extracting all the finger bones would we be able to analyse the ends of the fingers to see if any of the bone was missing – another symptom of leprosy. We would have to proceed very cautiously, making sure that a missing digit was not the result of momentary archaeological carelessness.

It had also become apparent that we were dealing with more than one body. From the evidence we had unearthed so far, it appeared that at least four or five corpses had been lowered into the burial site. At this stage, Robin was keen to suggest a possible criminal connection. It was a medieval tradition that criminals were buried at county boundaries; these were the dumping places for unfortunates who were not entitled to receive a Christian burial. This site, near a major crossing point of the River Tamar, could be just such a site. Robin had also begun to dismiss the likelihood of a battle burial, particularly because the skeleton that we had brought up was a female. In addition, the lack of any artefacts or records of a burial made a leprosy or criminal connection a much better bet.

As Day Two drew to a close, our search for the buildings seemed fruitless. Stuart suggested that the construction of the sewage farm might have obliterated the hospital, and in the last few minutes of our work that day, this view received unexpected support. A member of the Cornwall Archaeological Unit had taken a wander through the flower beds at the sewage farm and, in among the daffodils, had found pieces of early medieval pottery! When further research revealed that no 'foreign' soil had been brought in to create these beds, we knew that we had our first pieces of pottery contemporary with the lepers!

Day Three

Our focus was now the sewage farm. Nick Johnson had been examining the aerial photographs that had been periodically taken of the site since the early part of the century, and he had noticed that one small area had remained undeveloped. Massive tanks, offices and sheds had been built all over the rest of the sewage works, but just to one side of the road, there was a grassy lawn that appeared to have been left untouched.

John and his team immediately set to work here, and soon revealed something that might be a wall. Was it possible that some trace of the lepers might still exist? After two hours of excavation, we had part of our answer – medieval pottery *in situ*. Then, in the afternoon, a few pieces of stonework and some cobbling – perhaps part of a gate or entranceway – were found and in association with pottery from the correct period!

Our excavations in the small enclosure had led to no further burials, but Margaret's work on our female skeleton, now completely lifted from the trench, had revealed more. On one side of the dead woman's skull were a series of 'scourge marks' – scorings across the temple. One of the White Company knew of a medieval document that showed a surgeon cutting a person's head in just this place, presumably to relieve the pressure of an abscess. Had this woman been suffering from leprosy? It was difficult for Margaret to say one way or the other. Although we had discovered some of the classic symptoms – including some calcium reabsorption in the finger bones – the verdict would have to remain open.

One intriguing question remained – how long had this woman been buried here? The acidity of the soil was pertinent. Acid soil has a detrimental effect on bones, and since our skeleton's bones were in good condition, this could mean that the burial was a relatively recent one. However, medieval corpses were often limed – that is, sprinkled with caustic lime to aid decomposition – especially if they were diseased. If this were the case here, the lime might have neutralised the acidity and thus the skeleton might be older. To resolve this question, we extracted a bone to be carbon dated.

Our last act was to rebury the rest of the skeletal remains with an appropriate Christian service in the graveyard of a Launceston church. The irony was that, if our woman had been a leper, she would never have been granted this privilege at the time of her death, but now – centuries later – she had finally made it!

Final thoughts from Mick

Launceston was a good example of how you have to be very careful when you make an archaeological find – especially if it is a skeleton. In this case, there were always several possible explanations – lepers, Civil War casualties or executed prisoners. The evidence in the ground was difficult, so the explanation of lepers was not straightforward; radio carbon dating would give us the date, yet this still might not solve the riddle. But then that's archaeology!

Postscript

After the filming of TIME TEAM's work at Launceston, the bone that we took from the female skeleton was sent to the United States for carbon dating. The results are due shortly and will be revealed on the programme.

The skull found at Launceston, showing the 'scourge marks' on one temple. *(Mick Aston)*

GOVAN

GLASGOW

WHAT MIGHT HAVE HAPPENED

The great day had come and the magnificent stone coffin was rolled on logs into the building. The stonemasons admired the work even though it was not their own. The figure of the hunting man carried the spirit of the ancient carvers, and the stonemasons knew that the arrival of such a piece heralded an increase in the status of the site, which would mean more work for them. The MacAlpins had worked their magic and restored, at least for a while, some peace between the heathen Vikings and the local Britons. A respite from hostilities would mean more time to carve new stones.

Computer reconstruction of the face-shaped pot found at Govan.

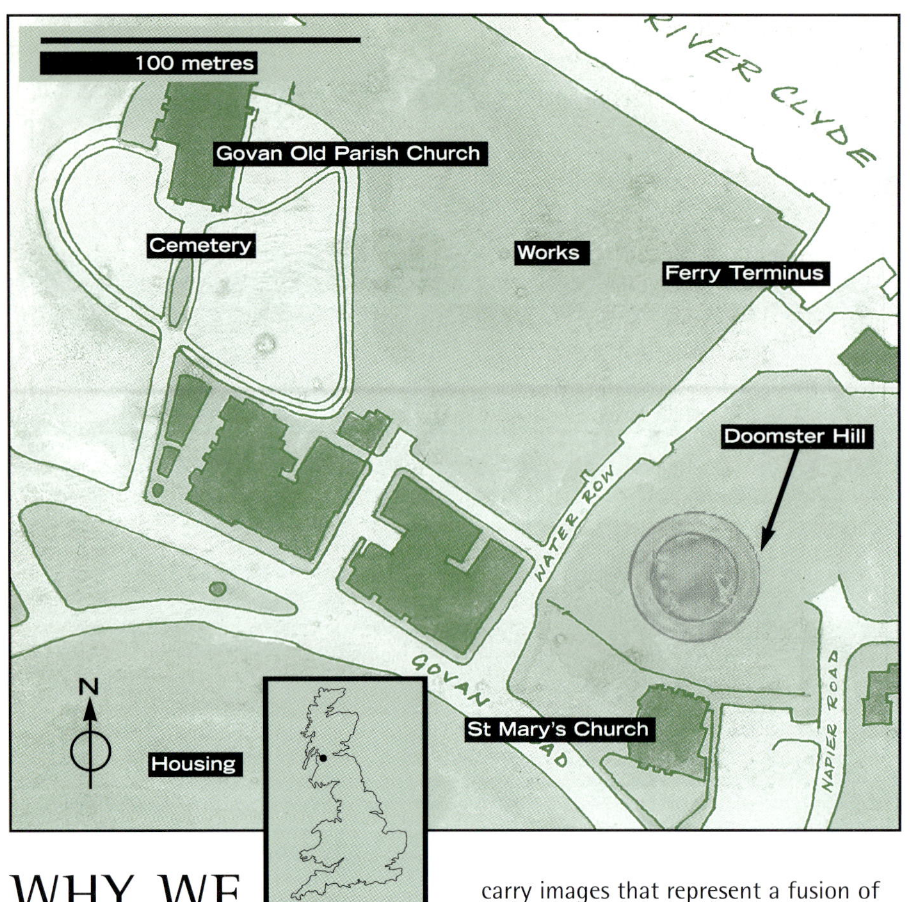

WHY WE WENT THERE

When we arrived in Govan, an ancient ship-building port on the River Clyde near Glasgow, we were faced by two pieces of evidence that stood out from the generally confusing Celtic twilight of early Scottish history. One was the presence in Govan's 18th-century church of one of the finest collections of ancient carved stones in Scotland. The other was the oval, or curvilinear, shape of the church's graveyard boundary – a shape usually taken to date from an early period.

The stones in the church are magnificent – over 31 burial stones from the 9th to 11th centuries, including early Christian cross slabs dating to the end of the 9th century, five 'hogback' grave markers of Scandinavian influence and a stone sarcophagus.

These stones reflect the influence of the many cultures that have battled for supremacy in this part of the world. It's as though there was a school of masons who, as the centuries passed, became adept at creating new styles in response to the latest influx of raiders. The stones carry images that represent a fusion of Celtic (seen in the ringed crosses), Early English (the interlaced patterns), Norse (the hogbacks) and Pictish (the carvings of horsemen and beasts).

A major monument in the church is a beautiful sarcophagus bearing a carved picture of a nobleman with a sword hunting an animal. When it was discovered in 1855, 1 metre (3 ft) below the surface, by a sexton digging in the graveyard, it had no cover and contained no bones. In 1908, it was moved inside the church. Was this the focus of a cult centre dedicated to St Constantine (to whom the present church was historically dedicated), or was it the tomb of one of the early kings of Strathclyde – possibly a member of the MacAlpin family, a number of whom took the name Constantine?

The hogback stones here comprise one of the largest collections in Britain and represent the houses of the dead. The name 'hogback' comes from the curved ridge of a roof-shaped structure that can have both tiles and, at each end, carvings of animals. This style of gravestone is associated with parts of northern Britain where there was Scandinavian settlement. Interestingly, there is no equivalent in Scandinavia itself.

Alongside these essentially pagan monuments are the early Christian cross slabs and the cross shafts, as well as one example of a sun stone carving that could be the earliest Christian stone in the collection. At the bottom of it is a carving of a horseman in Pictish style, and the 'sun' is actually a degenerate form of the snake-and-boss design (in which a number of snakes head out from a central boss), which is thought to date from the 8th century. Similar designs on Iona – the island in the Inner

Aerial view of Govan Church, with Trench 1 visible near the church and Trench 3 at the entrance. *(Carenza Lewis)*

Hebrides where St Columba established a monastery in AD 563 – date to this period, and as an illustration, it appears in the 8th-century *Book of Kells*.

So how should this collection be interpreted? The site has long been regarded as ancient, and in the atlas created by the mapmaker Blaeu in 1654, it is referred to as an important ecclesiastical establishment. There is also a suggestion that the ancient name for Govan – 'Meckle Govan' – refers to a small but prominent hill ('govan') of high status ('meckle'). Yet historians disagree about its early origins. In his book *The Early Christian Monuments of Govan and Inchinnan*, C A Ralegh Radford asserts that Govan was founded as a home for the relics of St Constantine, a relatively minor Celtic saint, when their original resting place at Kintyre became vulnerable to Viking attack. However, Alan MacQuarrie, TIME TEAM's consultant on historical Scottish documents, regards the site as a cult centre set up by the MacAlpin dynasty to legitimise their rule. A third view put forward by our guest expert, archaeologist Anna Ritchie, was that this site was an important burial ground for the kings of Strathclyde.

However, but for the presence of the stones, there is little evidence for an early Christian site here. Glasgow, only three miles from Govan, already had an important and well-documented shrine to St Kentigern, which, from early in the 7th century, would have been a powerful focus for a Christian settlement. Kentigern (*c.* AD 518–603) – also known as St Mungo, who was the first bishop of Glasgow and founded the cathedral there – is certainly a more important and clearly discernible figure in early Christianity than Constantine. The dedication of the site to the latter may, as Macquarrie suggests, simply have been an act of political expediency by the MacAlpin dynasty.

The MacAlpins played an important part in Govan's history. In the 8th and 9th centuries, various factions battled for power, the Anglo-Danish settlers on the mainland and the pagan Norsemen, . The MacAlpin dynasty was one of the few forces capable of imposing a settlement between them. In AD 870, a Viking army led by Olaf the White, the King of Dublin, and the intriguingly named Ivar the Boneless besieged Dumbarton Rock, the chief fortress of the Strathclyde Britons, which controls entry to the upper Clyde and Govan. They defeated Arthgal, the king of Strathclyde, who was killed in 872 at the request of Constantine I, son of Kenneth Mac Alpin, King of the Scots. (The term Scots here has to be seen in the context of the MacAlpins having their power base in both Ireland and Scotland.) By the 10th century – perhaps the period of our earliest stones – the Strathclyde kings were dominated by the MacAlpin family, and it seems highly coincidental that the name of one of their great kings, Constantine II (r. 900–952), was identical to the dedication of the Govan church. Was Govan founded to justify and sanctify the domination of the MacAlpins? Who was buried in the sarcophagus?

Faced with a variety of historical

COMPARITIVE STRATIGRAPHY

The depth at which finds are unearthed may not determine their age. This becomes clear when a site's stratigraphy – the order and relative positions of different strata in the soil – is studied. *(A)* A church wall is built on top of foundations. Inside the church, a floor is laid, and outside is a grassy churchyard. Grave 1 is probably the same date as the church as it cuts into the same ground surface, but it may predate the church. *(B)* Over time, a soil layer builds up against the wall in the churchyard, and a variety of floors are laid in the church. Grave 2, which cuts through the built-up soil, must have been dug while the wall was still standing but some time after it was constructed. *(C)* The church has fallen down and the wall has been reduced to a heap of rubble overlying the below-soil-level wall, the church floors and the wall foundations. Soil has accumulated on top of all this. Grave 3 has been cut through this soil layer, and must be later in date than the collapse of the wall.

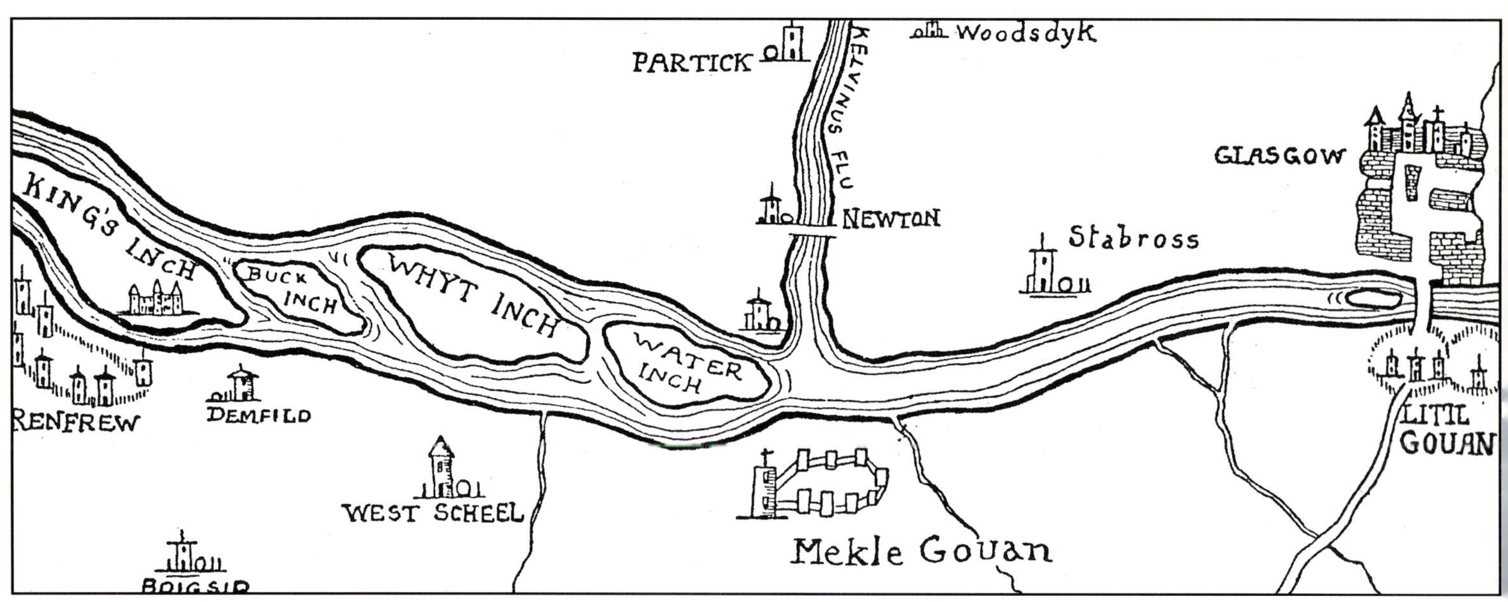

opinions based on the interpretation of ancient texts, it was something of a relief to tackle the archaeological evidence. However, this would be the first time that we would have to do without Mick, who had broken his leg while searching for a holy well in Wales. Although we were able to put a link through to him by telephone, Tony and the whole team felt his absence keenly.

In Govan, we would be working with Steve Driscoll and his team from Glasgow University. In 1995, GUARD – the Glasgow University Archaeological Research Division – had excavated two areas of the site. One near the current church had revealed, as might be expected, a series of demolition layers relating to earlier churches. At the lower levels of this excavation were discovered a number of unmortared stones. Could these be the foundations of the earliest timber building on the site? Any early Christian site here would have been surrounded by a wall, or *vallum*, and the present shape of the graveyard wall – an oval or pear shape – would seem to indicate this. In the second area that they investigated, close to this wall, the Glasgow excavators had found the remains of a number of workshops, some of which contained early medieval material including worked shale. This may have been an industrial area associated with an early site.

Time had not permitted GUARD to extend their search further. They had hoped to look for evidence of an entranceway into the enclosure, and they had focused their attention on the pointed end of the pear shape. This headed in the direction of another key element to the site. A number of documents from the 17th and 18th centuries refer to the existence of a large artificial mound called locally *'Doomster Hill'*, acorruption of the Scots word 'dempster', meaning 'law giver'. It had been suggested that this might be an early 'moot hill' – a place where the king and his followers met to make laws and dispense justice. Excavation in 1965 had revealed what might be part of a ditch, but little pottery was found that would enable a date to be determined. If an early moot hill could be found to have existed from a period related to the carved stones, this would reinforce the impression of the whole site having been a highly important ecclesiastical and royal administrative centre.

This site now presented a range of obstacles. First, the graveyard had been in use until the 19th century, and we would have to be careful not to disturb any late burials. Second, shipyard buildings and a dye works had once occupied the Doomster Hill site, and the excavation we planned would have to be large enough to enable great amounts of industrial debris to be removed safely. To overcome the first problem, we chose to extend the excavation along the route of a path that crossed the graveyard. This would hopefully avoid any recent burials.

We would have three targets for the weekend. The first was to relocate the early unmortared stone in the graveyard, and extend that excavation further to see if we could lfind any walls or other evidence of a building. The second was to excavate at the pointed end of the

(Top) Blaeu's map of 1654, showing Meckle Govan' as an important ecclesiastical site.
(Above) Dumbarton Rock and the River Clyde. *(Carenza Lewis)*

that required a trench 14 metres (46 ft) wide and 3 metres (10 ft) deep – our biggest yet! – which would involve removing the recent industrial layers and post-medieval material. It was going to take a day before any results showed up.

Phil and Steve had established a site for Trench 3, hoping to find some kind of entranceway. It was also possible that, if an important ecclesiastical site and a moot hill had existed at the same time, there may have been a ceremonial route between them. Before excavation could begin, Phil had to remove the concrete slabs that formed a pathway round the graveyard.

Govan's vicar, Tom Davidson Kelly, was on hand to show Robin, Tony and archaeologist Anna Ritchie around the stones and, in particular, the magnificent sarcophagus. The absence of a cross suggested to Robin that the stone coffin had been created for a secular rather than a Christian purpose – the hunting scene seemed a typical pursuit of a nobleman – but Tom felt that a Christian interpretation could be placed on the scene: a Christian preacher out hunting for unconverted souls. However, the imagery certainly seemed more pagan than this interpretation allowed for.

By now, Stuart had had a chance to look around the site and had as usual come to his own conclusions. According to him, the location and shape of pear shape to see if an entranceway could be found and to unearth any finds that might indicate an early date. And finally, we were going to excavate the Doomster Hill site to see if we could locate a ditch and find material that might help to date the site. We also planned to recreate a carved stone to allow Phil to observe stone-carving skills.

Day One

In our first excavation, we could clearly see the foundation rubble of the later, post-medieval Govan churches. If we could find a corner of the wall below this, we might be able to see an alignment – if this was east–west, it would indicate a Christian origin. As this trench progressed, we had a chance to bring in the stone for our carving experiment. Local stone carver Barry GroVe was going to tackle this, after Victor had transferred his design from paper on to the stone. Using references from other stones, metalwork and sources such as the *Book of Kells*, we planned to create a stone that combined a number of influences, including Norse figures and interlacing.

By the afternoon of Day One, we had encountered our first body – it was disarticulated (with bones unattached at the joints) so it had probably been moved aside or damaged by a late burial. Ancient graveyards contain layer upon layer of bodies, and when new graves are dug, they may go into two or three earlier levels of corpses. The presence of a shroud pin indicated that this was a relatively recent burial, sometime in the last 200 to 300 years. After careful recording, this was removed for reburial.

Robin and Carenza had now had a chance to look at the earliest maps of the area drawn by Blaeu in 1654. It showed 'Meckle Govan' and a mound that might relate to our moot hill, the site of our second excavation. Steve Driscoll had devised an excavation plan

(Top) Computer realisation of the moot hill theory for Doomster Hill. The moot hill would have been on the left, with a processional way connecting it to the ecclesiastical site on the right. *(Above)* Computer reconstruction of a wall of the first, wooden church at Govan, showing the foundations. *(Inset)* What was initially thought to be a post-hole near the church. *(Carenza Lewis)*

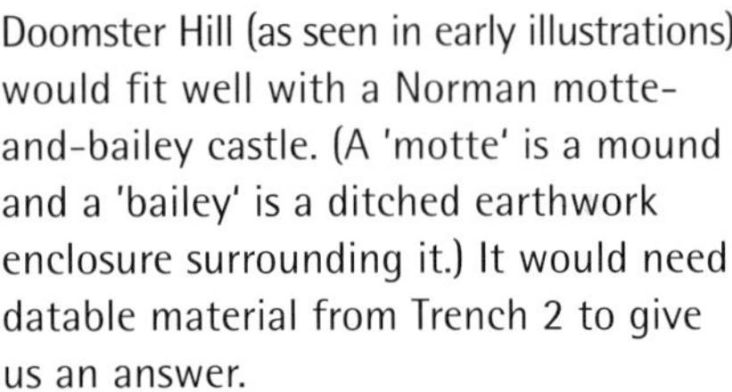

Doomster Hill (as seen in early illustrations) would fit well with a Norman motte-and-bailey castle. (A 'motte' is a mound and a 'bailey' is a ditched earthwork enclosure surrounding it.) It would need datable material from Trench 2 to give us an answer.

Day One ended with a trip to Dumbarton Rock, the 'impregnable' fortress of the kings of Strathclyde that had been raided by the Vikings in AD 870. The name 'Dumbarton' is derived from *Dun Breatann* – 'the fortress of the Britons'. A volcanic plug of basalt that dominates the Clyde estuary, it has the longest recorded history of any such stronghold in Britain. *The Annals of Ulster* of AD 658 refer to a 'King of Clyde Rock', and Bede mentions it in his *Ecclesiastical History of the English Church*, completed in AD 731. The rock was crucial to the control of the western seaways. Much of its early history has been destroyed, although two gravestones with interlaced ornament from the 10th and 11th centuries were found there.

Day Two

Saturday in Govan is market day, and this has been traditionally held on the moot hill site. Shoppers and market traders surrounded our excavation, which had become a major operation – already 1.5 metres (5 ft) deep and heading deeper.

Stuart's views on the moot hill had become progressively more certain. The importance of this crossing point and the existence of many motte-and-baileys in the region should have led to the siting of a castle here. The shape of the hill in an early illustration had a striking similarity to a nearby hill called Dim Vim Motte. Stuart was excited by the possibility that this could be a major undocumented castle site.

Trench 1 was now becoming increasingly complicated. Carenza, with the help of members of the GUARD team, had discovered at least three grave-cuts (where the soil shows the difference between the infilled grave and the earth surrounding it), one of which contained 14th-century pottery. Had these graves been cut when an early church was still standing? If we could find a grave that respected the early non-mortared stone wall line, that would help.

Meanwhile, our stone carving was proceeding well. Victor's design, drawn in charcoal, had been traced with paint and now it was being 'scribed' – outlined by sharp cuts to provide a permanent record before carving began.

Geophysics had at last got into action in what was for them very unpromising territory. Graveyards are one vast area of disturbance. Gravestones, trenches, cobbles, tree stumps – all these and more can interfere with any signals. However, we might be able to find some of the older burial areas in some of the gaps that appear on a 19th-century map. In 1899, Sir John Maxwell had located 46 stone monuments at Govan and had drawn a plan of their locations. There was just a chance that some of the missing 15 were still lying undiscovered in the graveyard. Back in the incident room, which had been set up in a church building at the edge of the boundary wall, John had located on the computer printout what appeared to be a set of 'blobs' against the boundary. Could these be one of the missing stones?

In Trench 1, a more recent burial had hampered progress, but we also had a bit of encouragement in the form of a face-shaped pot. About 600 years old, this is one of the nicest objects we have found on TIME TEAM, and we were able to get Victor to reconstruct what the original might have looked like when it was new.

Stuart had now begun to have doubts about the curvilinear boundary wall. On a 1750 survey by General Roy, the boundary was rectilinear, and John's geophysics seemed to be showing the edge of a square boundary. Unfortunately, this was in the part of the graveyard with the most burials, and in the time left, the team felt that an excavation that would probably require removing recent burials could not be undertaken. John offered another survey using deeper probing signals to locate the depth of the rectilinear boundary. We hoped that this would show whether it was, in fact, a later feature, but subsequently, the results were not clear enough to prove the case one way or the other.

Excavations at the entrance point had also proved frustrating, with little datable evidence, and it became clear that we would have to extend the digging. Stuart felt that we were a metre or two away from

(Above left) The stone carving created by Barry Grove. *(Carenza Lewis)*
(Above right) The carving being painted with ochre. *(Sue Francis, Creative TV Facilities)*

across the river.

Barry Grove's work on his stone was now complete. The monument was finished by having the incised background areas painted in ochre, as was the tradition with such stones. The results were spectacular.

In Trench 1, we had discovered more of the unmortared stone walls that remain the earliest features on this site. Lack of a grave or other finds contemporary with them means that the exact date and identification of the building remain a mystery. As Mick said in his telephone call to Tony, archaeology tend to throw up the unexpected and you have to respond to that.

In the end, Stuart's work on Doomster Hill and the rest of the team's work with GUARD to interpret that site were our main contributions from the weekend – and, of course, the beautifully carved and painted stone, which we left as a gift for the church and the people of Govan.

the last recorded entrance point.

Our search for the missing stones proved to be an exciting but fruitless quest – John's blobs turned out to be 18th- and 19th-century grave slabs. In Trench 2 at Doomster Hill, work had progressed despite the alternative attraction of an England/Scotland football match being played that afternoon. Mick Worthington, a member of the TIME TEAM digging team, and the GUARD diggers had found the edge of what might prove to be a ditch. Only more excavation would answer our questions.

Joined by Phil, Barry Grove had started chiselling away the stone. It was interesting to note that the tools used to carve our slab had changed little since Roman times. Barry told us of the constant need for itinerant blacksmiths, who had to accompany stonemasons to keep their tools sharp.

Day Two ended with the short-lived idea that one of Carenza's grave-cuts might actually be a post-hole. If this contained early pottery at its base, we might have an early structure.

Day Three

We had now extended our entrance trench excavation, which at an early stage appeared to be more positive. A layer of stone and gravel, which may indicate a path, had begun to appear.

Mick and the GUARD team in Trench 2, joined by Phil, had at last located a substantial assemblage of pottery shards, including a base. The ditch was now marked by two different colours of sand, and the edge of the mound showed a series of what Phil called 'tip lines' – the faint lines that occur between each layer of material used to build up a mound. In the end, the TIME TEAM concluded that, from the evidence, this was more likely to have been a motte-and-bailey than a moot hill. No find appeared dating from earlier than the 13th or 14th century, and this tended to support Stuart's theory that we had located the site of a major undocumented castle. However, Steve Driscoll disagreed. To him, the pronounced terrace halfway up the hill, and the origins of the hill's name ('law giver') both indicated a moot hill. He also questioned the neccessity for a castle here when one was already sited

Final thoughts from Mick

I was sorry to miss Govan – it was just after I broke my leg in north Wales! I was particularly looking forward to seeing all the sculptured stones, which is one of my interests, and also Dumbarton Rock, which is a site I have long wanted to visit. Anyway, the rest of the team managed without me, so no one is indispensable!

Top) The fragment of the face-shaped pot, showing the face, which was found in Trench 1. *(Carenza Lewis)*
(Bottom) Computer realisation of the motte-and-bailey theory for Doomster Hill at Govan.

MALTON

NORTH YORKSHIRE

WHAT MIGHT HAVE HAPPENED

With his king and the court due for a visit, the baron was concerned that the castle should look its best. A close watch was being kept for any signs of the troublesome Scots; he wanted nothing to disturb the peace, at least for the next few days. In the kitchens, there was a frenzy of activity. A pig was being roasted and new pottery vessels laid out, including a magnificent new water jug with two frogs guarding its spout.

Computer reconstruction of the castle at Malton, with the freestanding medieval building within its walls.

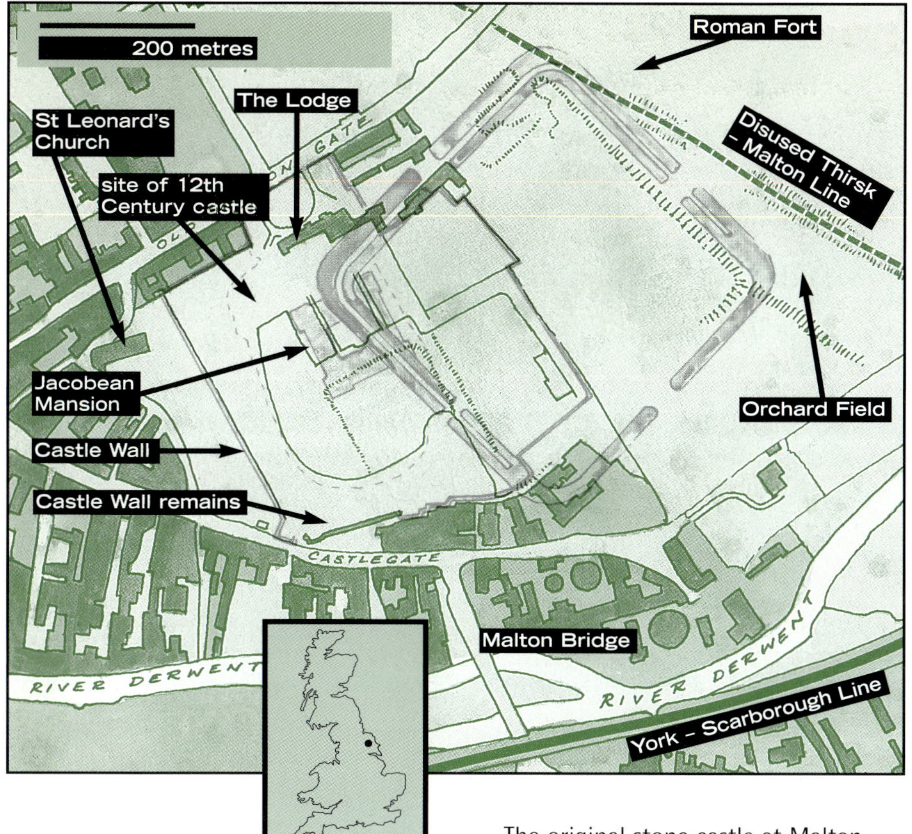

WHY WE WENT THERE

Malton in North Yorkshire is situated halfway between York and the coast. It commands a crucial route north – a crossing point of the River Derwent – and has been the site of many battles and disputes over its vital position. The town was the site of an important market throughout the Middle Ages, and there is a Gilbertine priory located on the outskirts.

The Romans built a fort here at the hub of a system of roads, and Roman Malton – called *Derventio* – was an important strategic site. The fort has been excavated and can now be seen as a series of grassed-over humps and bumps east of the castle site. By comparison, not much is known about the prehistoric settlement that preceded it, nor about the later Anglo-Saxon occupation. The Norman castle here was destroyed and rebuilt a number of times during the Middle Ages. There is still a massive wall – marked on maps as 'Castle Wall' - whose date was uncertain before TIME TEAM's arrival. Otherwise little seems to have survived.

The original stone castle at Malton - which may have been preceded by a motte-and-bailey (*see* page 28) – had two advantages that would secure it into the Middle Ages and beyond. First, the castle builders had recognised, as had the Romans before them, that the position was a strategic one and so had sited their fortress accordingly. Second, they had had a plentiful supply of building material from both the remains of the Roman fort and a local outcrop of limestone. Henry I (r 1110–1135) granted the original land to Eustace FitzJohn, and it is likely that the castle builders took advantage of the large ditch that may have been part of the motte-and-bailey, as well as possibly some of the fortifications of the Roman fort.

The site's later history includes the building of a Jacobean house and lodge, which, according to a work by a local painter, once had extensive grounds and gardens. The lodge itself still survives and is owned by Norris Binner who, before turning the building into a hotel, wanted to find out what might lie beneath his garden. The area of the castle and the Roman fort belongs to Ryedale District Council, who want to create a public park here to coincide with the Millennium. It was an invitation from them and from Mr Binner that brought us to Malton.

Day One

Our work on the site involved us in close consultations with English Heritage, and their local inspector John Ette had agreed to oversee our activities. This site is scheduled, which means that a number of strict criteria had to be agreed before we would be allowed access. Scheduling a site is supposed to protect the material in the ground; the relevant legislation, which is enforced by penalties, was framed in favour of the preservation of the physical archaeology. The fact that a site such as Malton is being preserved on the basis of little information is irrelevant to the scheduling process, and despite the greatly appreciated assistance of John Ette and local archaeologists, we were extremely lucky to have persuaded the Secretary of State to allow us access.

This access was limited, restricting our investigations to just five trenches of a set size. At each stage, John Ette would have to be consulted and his approval gained.

On our first morning, our attention had focused on the raised banks that seemed to create a square platform in the area thought to contain the castle. These were the most obvious features, but were they medieval, part of a Jacobean garden or even a section of the Roman fort? There were some differences of opinion among the team members, but they all had time to ruminate while workers, kindly supplied by the council, cleared the site, which was entirely covered in shoulder-high nettles.

Phil was concerned about the trees near our projected first trench. Trees can be easily damaged if too many of their delicate surface roots, as well as their more obvious roots, are cut. In addition, it was his contention that, of the two banks we had as options, one was easier to get at. However, Mick felt that the other bank, aligned with the edge of the castle wall, might be a better archaeological bet, and with the nettles now disposed of, this was finally agreed.

Meanwhile, Beric Morley, our buildings expert, and Carenza had ventured off into the garden of a neighbouring house to look at what on the map appeared to be remains of one of the castle walls. With so many phases of castle building on this site, we doubted that any feature could be found to date this wall. However, Beric came to our rescue and was able to identify the small buttresses on the outside of the wall as 'early' – possibly 11th or 12th century – and he also spotted the remains of a medieval garderobe, or toilet shaft.

This was excellent news. As our first trench was above this area, it seemed possible that we might find features associated with this period and even with the castle itself. As this excavation progressed, it became clear that we were dealing with a vast ditch that had once lain behind the walls. We also had found small amounts of Roman pottery! Could this be an extension of the Roman fort, or had this debris simply spread into a medieval feature?

Mick, handicapped by a plastered leg, was still able to survey the team's work with the help of Nick Corcos, one of his research students. Using a camera connected remotely to a close-circuit television, Nick walked through the site while the series' archaeological consultant directed him from the comfort of TIME TEAM's four-wheel drive.

John and Chris, now with a reasonable amount of cleared land to work with, had begun to survey the flat area between the walls and the Jacobean lodge. The local council were keen to get an idea of all the archaeological features within this, to use them as part of the projected park's design. This was also critical to the success of their application for lottery funding.

While this got underway, Robin was able to supply the team with Malton's historical background. This included visits by Richard I in about 1194 and Edward II in c. 1307 and an occupation by Robert Bruce, who used it as a military base in 1322. During the reign of King John (1199–1216), the castle was 'slighted' – made militarily useless by having its walls pulled down, any wooden structures within them burned and other damage done – but it was later rebuilt.

The history of the later Jacobean lodge was equally complex. Built in 1604 by Ralph, Lord Eure, at the beginning of the reign of James I, it – and the house to which it belonged – are regarded by

some experts as being in the style of the so-called 'prodigy houses', designed as displays of wealth and power. In 1632, Eure's mansion, a stronghold of the Roman Catholic faith at a time when this was unpopular (*see* p. 5), was bombarded by the local sheriff's artillery. In 1675, it fell victim to a dispute between Margaret and Mary, the daughters of William, the second son of Lord Eure, who had inherited the property. Unable to agree on ownership, the sisters took the case to law, and with no obvious solution to the dispute in sight after about two decades, the local high sheriff, Henry Marwood, ordered the house to be dismantled stone by stone, leaving only the lodge standing!

With slow progress being made in Trench 1 and no clear geophysics targets yet emerging, it was decided to place another evaluation trench in the bank on the Malton side of the castle grounds, just where Phil had originally wanted to dig. This might locate the 'return' of our ditch – where it bent round to follow the contour of the hill – and more of what appeared to be a stone structure in Trench 1.

Day Two

With John Ette's permission, we had decided to extend Trench 1 further into the platform, and even at a fairly early stage, this appeared to have paid off. We began to locate large stones that

(Top right) The remains of the stone structure found in Trench 1. *(Mick Aston)*
(Top left) A posthumous engraving of Edward II, who visited Malton Castle in about 1307. *(Mary Evans Picture Library)*
(Above) The Lodge at Malton. Note the columns at the entrance, similar to ones found at another Yorkshire estate, Howley Hall. *(Mick Aston)*

might just be the edge of a freestanding building. Beric considered their shape and size to be appropriately medieval. Phil now had his chance to dig into the return bank of the feature that Trench 1 had picked up. Meanwhile, Mick and Robin explored Malton's market, with Robin pushing Mick from street to street in his wheelchair.

During the reign of Henry II (1154–89), there was an expansion of activity as Old Malton – which was north of the Roman fort and had developed from the previous Romano-British settlement that later became centred on a mill and a pre-Conquest church – fell into disuse and New Malton grew up around the castle. References quoted in the *Victoria County History* speak of an influx of weavers, goldsmiths and masons. There was no other market town in the vicinity to rival Malton, and its growing importance was confirmed by the construction of a town wall at some point in the late medieval period. By the time John Leland, the King's Antiquary, visited the town in the reign of Henry VIII (1509–47), he was able to write of a thriving market here. Remnants of the medieval street plan can still be seen today.

Mr Binner, obviously keen for us to explore under his garden, had a hunch that the mansion still lay beneath the orchard behind the lodge. Stewart had looked at a number of possible models for this Jacobean mansion, and Howley Hall in Yorkshire seemed the closest bet. It had a very similar gatehouse, with the same arrangement of columns at the entrance. According to Beric, such estates were arranged in nine symmetrical squares, and this resembled the existing layout of Mr Binner's lodge and garden, as well as suggesting yet another estate – this time, Wollaton Hall near Nottingham. Stewart had surveyed the likely dimensions of the mansion on the ground, which placed our main target in the middle of the overgrown orchard. Ryedale Council's team of workmen were once again called into action.

As John Ette and Stewart both felt that we should not excavate before the area had had a geophysical survey, Mick and Carenza took this opportunity to study Malton's layout and the relationship between the castle, the market and the town. When combined with the abbey,

Computer reconstruction of the Jacobean mansion, lodge and gardens at Malton.

these comprised a typical set of features found in medieval towns. The castle served to protect the market, whose location at the crossroads of so many routes allowed it to flourish. It was clear from aerial photographs of Malton that the ancient road that had once surrounded the market and formed the walled boundary could still be traced.

We were also able to watch one of the key weapons of the medieval period being made. Barry Scott, our bladesmith, had agreed to work with Phil to make an iron sword in a local blacksmith's forge. Phil was surprised at the ease with which the red hot metal could be pounded into a square bar, but the real skill came in the final beating-out process. The sword was completed by the addition of a crossbar and round pommel.

By the end of Day Two, we had at last cleared Mr Binner's orchard, and John and Chris's results had given us a possible target. Stewart would have to make the final decision the next day. Trench 2, in the woods nearest the town, had revealed a mortared base that could be the return of a wall, and in Trench 3, we had begun to unearth significant amounts of late medieval material. Beric was particularly excited by the discovery of part of an aquamanile – a decorated water jug that he said would have graced a 'posh' medieval table. The pieces of pot and other material that we had found suggested that we were in the demolition layer of a medieval building – perhaps part of the castle destroyed in the 15th or 16th century.

Day Three

This was the moment of reckoning for Stewart. On the computer printout, John had showed him what appeared to be a wall, but was it the inside or outside of the mansion? If we placed a trench inside the wall, we might just get the courtyard. With John Ette satisfied with the location of our fourth trench, we began to clear back the topsoil. After two to three hours of excavation, this revealed a crumbled plaster layer that looked like the floor of our Jacobean house. Two finds confirmed Stewart's guess: one was a piece of window lead typical of the period, and the other, more excitingly, was the fragment of a mullion, or stone window frame. This building had appeared exactly where Beric, Stewart and Mr Binner had predicted, and we were delighted and relieved to have located it.

John and Chris, carrying out a geophysical survey of the area where the gardens of the mansion should have been located, had come up with what looked like a definite structure. Here, we were close to the Roman fort's gateway and also not far from the castle, so great care had to be taken. However, John Ette and the team finally decided that our fifth trench, a small one, should be placed over John and Chris's mysterious feature. Yet excavation had no sooner begun than it came to a halt. From the evidence of small pieces of pottery – probably flowerpots – it appeared that we had begun to uncover the formal gardens of the mansion. Given the scheduling restrictions, these could not be removed in order to look at what might lie below!

This was a frustrating but archaeologically correct conclusion, and it raised interesting questions for all of the team about the relative importance of different archaeological features. On the site of Trench 5, we might well have had a Roman structure, on top of which lay a medieval building, on top of which were Jacobean gardens. What is the important level of archaeology that you excavate down to? It could be argued that, with more time, a careful excavation of a small section of the Jacobean garden would have given us access to a portion of what lay below. However, as John Ette reminded us, the bias of scheduling is in favour of preservation, not investigation.

Still, to have located the castle and the freestanding medieval building was quite an achievement, and the pottery, fragments of building material (including medieval glass), lead fishing weights and other finds we had dug up would have pride of place in the Malton museum. Along with the discovery of the mansion and its gardens, we had been able to fill in some of the post-Roman detail of what had previously been something of an archaeological blank slate.

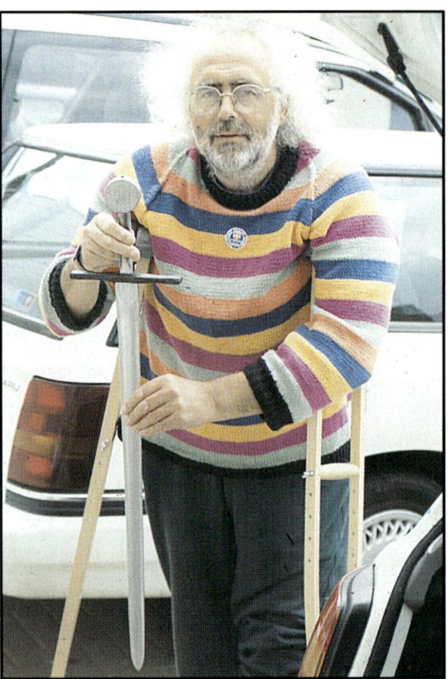

Final thoughts from Mick

I was still very immobile at Malton, and it made me fully appreciate the difficulties physically disabled people have in getting around ancient monuments.

It is not uncommon to have Romano-British, medieval and post-medieval sites mixed up together, and the Malton site showed this well. It is particularly difficult to aim to investigate one period alone, and this proved the case here. Nevertheless, much was learned about the castle, and the details of the Jacobean mansion were of great interest.

(Left) Some of the finds unearthed from Trench 3. *(Carenza Lewis)*
(Right) Mick, on cruthches, holding the iron sword made for TIME TEAM by bladesmith Barry Scott. *Mick Aston)*

NETHERAVON

WILTSHIRE

WHAT MIGHT HAVE HAPPENED

The administrator stood on the hillside and watched the final tiles being put into place. The patterned roof could be seen clearly from the other side of the valley, and the position he had chosen for the villa, overlooking the river, allowed him excellent views of the surrounding countryside. In the distance, he could see the cartloads of grain coming down from the Plain – it had been a good harvest and his returns meant that a beautiful mosaic floor could be created for the dining room. He looked forward to the feasts that he would enjoy there, and felt a sense of satisfaction at the advancement his family had achieved since the arrival of the Romans.

Computer reconstruction of what the Romano-British villa at Netheravon may have looked like, including the multi-coloured patterned roof.

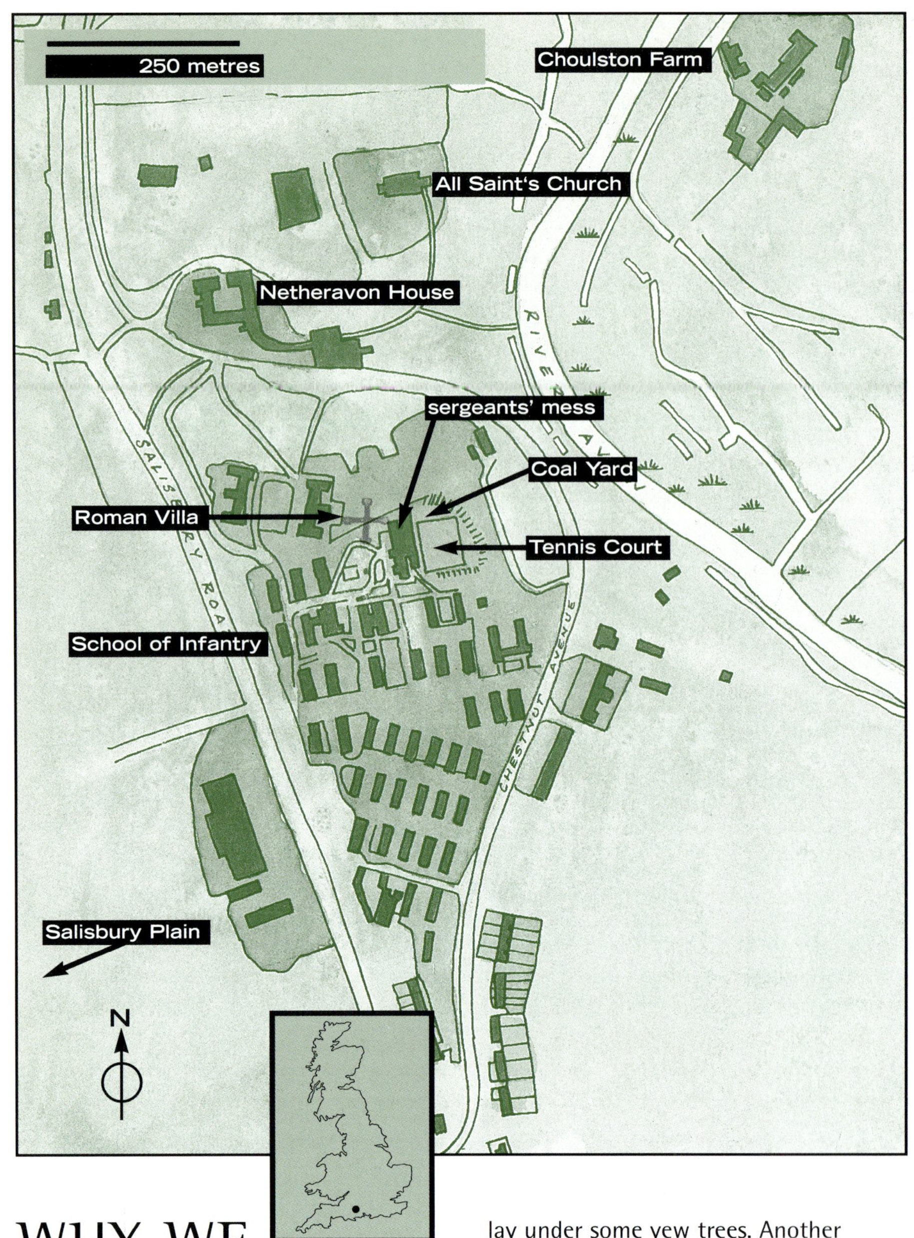

WHY WE WENT THERE

We came to Netheravon in Wiltshire with two important pieces of information.

In August 1907, Lieutenant Colonel William Hawley, an antiquarian and excavator of parts of Stonehenge, uncovered a tessellated pavement – a mosaic floor – on the site of the Netheravon military base, established three years earlier to train the cavalry. We know about this discovery from a report by Hawley in the *Wiltshire Archaeological Magazine*, describing his excavation and referring to the site as being 'about 100 yrds [91m] south of Netheravon House'. There was also the suggestion that the majority of a villa lay under some yew trees. Another report told of the unearthing of tessellated pavement at Netheravon, which came to light in 1936 when a sump was being dug in the coalyard of what was then the Small Arms School.

Hawley described the floor that he had found as consisting primarily of coarse red tesserae (mosaic pieces), with an inner border of white tesserae and four rows of plum-coloured ones. A few small patches of the mosaic appeared on top of what, he wrote, may have been an earlier floor of *opus signinum* – Roman concrete.

With the contraction of army training in Germany in recent years, Salisbury Plain is increasingly being used as one of the major army training centres in Britain. It is one of the largest areas of undeveloped chalkland in Europe and contains a huge number of prehistoric sites. Ironically, the presence of the army, whose activities have occasionally threatened sites, has served to protect the Plain from development. However, places such as Netheravon have been earmarked for future use by the army for training. And so the Wiltshire county archaeologist and the Ministry of Defence had asked us to come and find out what was there.

If Hawley's assumptions were correct, the site could contain an important Romano-British villa. Both Roy Canham, chief archaeological officer for the area, and Mark Corney, our expert on villas for the programme, had pointed out the advantageous topography at Netheravon. The hillside on which the site is situated, which commands a view over the flood plain of the Avon, would be a typical location for a villa. It was

(Top right) Lieutenant Colonel William Hawley, the first excavator at Netheravon, in about 1920. *(Citation)*
(Above) An example of a Roman tessellated pavement found in Britain. *(From;* Roman Mosaics in Britain. *David S Neal/©RCHME)*

Early concrete

It may be surprising to learn that concrete – a mixture of cement, stone, sand and water – is not a building material of relatively recent invention. In fact, the earliest use of concrete so far discovered was at Lepenski Vir in the former Yugoslavia, where it was employed for hut floors as long ago as *c.* 5600 BC. It was also used by the Egyptians in the building of the Great Pyramid at Giza in 2500 BC. In the 2nd century BC, the Romans accidently discovered how to produce 'possolanic cement' from lime and silica or aluminium oxide, and they later used this in concrete to construct aqueducts and amphitheatres. In AD 127, the walls of the Pantheon in Rome were built with a lightweight concrete, incorporating crushed pumice as aggregate.

With the fall of the Romans, the 'recipe' for superior concrete was lost, although in the Middle Ages, limestone mortar was employed to infill the walls of castles and in the building of cathedrals (mainly in foundations). It was only in 1756 that the first high-quality concrete since the Romans was produced, by John Smeaton for the rebuilding of the Eddystone lighthouse.

also quite common for the Britons, as they adopted the new ways of the invaders, to set up villas close to already existing Iron Age settlements, and one of these is known to have been nearby. Mark suggested that the period we were looking at was likely to be the 3rd or 4th century AD.

In addition, we knew that there had been quite a few vast Roman estates in this area, even though few of these have actually been located, and there is also a tradition of villas being sited close to the subsequent locations of churches and medieval town centres. The village of Netheravon appears in the *Domesday Book* of 1086 as 'Nigravre' or 'Nigra Avra', and it seems likely that traces of it would lie near the river. The parish church of All Saints, which appears to date from the 11th century, now stands in an isolated position next to Netheravon House, built in the 18th century. Could this important medieval community have had its origins in the previous existence of a Romano-British villa and and its associated settlements?

As with most antiquarian evidence, the picture was far from clear. No official report of the Roman finds was ever written – Hawley's report had come to us secondhand and partial. In 1914, Goddard, writing in his list of prehistoric antiquities, mentions Hawley's finds:

In the grounds of Netheravon House, Lt Colonel W Hawley and Rev G H Engleheart uncovered, 1907, a small room about 13ft [4 m] square, plainly paved with red and white tesserae, with not very definite wall foundations, the ground round seemed to have been disturbed and no extension could be found, and the work was never completed. A 'bath' 5ft x 5ft x 2ft [1.5 x 1.5 x 0.6m] deep is said to have adjoined the room.

This reference added two new details to the small amount of knowledge that we had about the Netheravon site: the name of the Reverend G H Engelheart, who, it seems, worked with Hawley, and the discovery of a 'bath'.

We had one additional piece of anecdotal evidence collected from a local source. A booklet on archaeological finds discovered in the area, published in 1968, says that the Hawley excavation took place

on the site of the present coalyard and Sergeants' Mess ... some of the local inhabitants who assisted these worthy gentlemen told me that a tessellated pathway was also revealed and it ran off from the excavated site in an easterly direction through the site of the present Sergeants' Mess.

So we had three key facts to aid our work: Hawley's measurement of a distance of 91 metres (100 yd) from Netheravon House, and two relatively modern structures - a coalyard and a sergeants' mess – identified as being near the archaeology. With the help of army plans, it seemed likely that we could locate these buildings. Hawley's reference to yew trees was less helpful. Since he had examined the area in 1907, the trees had grown and spread to become a broad strip between Netheravon House and the training camp, and we could no longer recognise the specific group he had used for identification.

Despite evidence of massive exploitation by the Romans of Salisbury Plain, relatively few villa sites have been discovered there. It may be that the land

(Above) The parish church of All Saints, Netheravon – once the hub of an important medieval community, but now isolated on Salisbury plain. *(Mick Aston)*
(Top) An Anglo-Saxon carving in the church entrance. *(Carenza Lewis)*

around the edge of the Plain, such as the Avon valley, was where the villas that controlled and administered the farming were located.

Day One

When we arrived on the site, we were faced by acres of building rubble, concrete foundations and tarmacked roads, interspersed with the odd patch of grass, trees and shrubs.

One advantage of the hardened surface was that it provided a perfect runway for Mick, who had been equipped with a motorised wheelchair to save his still plastered leg. A disadvantage was that it limited the extent of the geophysics work that John and Chris could carry out. They began early in the day in those few places where they could hope to get readings. The tennis court, close to where the officers' mess had once been, was the largest area of accessible ground.

Working closely with the local archaeological unit, the county archaeological expert Duncan Coe and the army archaeologist Stuart Barnes devised a fairly strict scheme to tackle the site, given its potential importance. This plan contained an element relatively new to TIME TEAM – test pitting. Having only an approximate idea of the location of the villa, test pits measuring 1 metre by 1 metre (3.3 ft x 3.3 ft) dug around the site would, we thought, enable us to identify the spread of Roman material.

The subsoil on the site turned out to consist of hard chalk and flints, which made digging the pits an arduous task. In addition, once the depth was below 0.3–0.6 metre (1–2 ft), the restricted dimensions inhibited the swinging of an axe or pick, and retrieving soil from the base of the pits was equally difficult. As a result, the test pits became perhaps the least popular form of archaeological investigation tackled by our digging teams in this series!

Our key measurement – Hawley's '100 yrds south of Netheravon House' – had to be determined, and Carenza and Duncan Coe negotiated the barbed wire to do this. This took us through the band of yew trees and towards the sergeants' mess area. We didn't know how accurate Hawley's 'south' was, but his approximate distance and the location of the coalyard and sergeants' mess – found on Ministry of Defence

Eating the Roman way

Roman food bore little similarity to the food we associate with the Italians today – pasta, tomatoes and garlic. True, olive oil was a main ingredient, but probably more important was a well-matured fish sauce called *liquamen*, imported largely from Spain and Gaul. This pungent substance was added to many cooked foods.

The Romans were deeply interested in food and had their own cookery writers. The most famous was Marcus Gavius Apicius, a nobleman and gourmet during the reign of the emperor Tiberius in the 1st century AD, who wrote *Of Culinary Matters*, one of the world's first cookbooks. This includes a selection of ideas on how to cook the humble dormouse, which was considered a delicacy. The dormice, having been fattened up in battery chicken-type conditions, were stuffed with meat, pine kernels and fish sauce.

(Top left) Netheravon barracks from the air. *(Carenza Lewis)*
(Top Right) Carenza's trench in the sergeants' mess. *(Mick Aston)*
(Above) Phil and Robin masquerading as Roman cooks. *(Mick Aston)*

plans, and which, coincidently, turned out to more or less south of the house – made us decide to place a trench in each of these two areas. In addition, the spread of the test pits we were digging formed a roughly circular pattern around the extremities of the site, and when geophysics located some features in the tennis court, this was also allocated test pits.

The trench nearest the coalyard produced our first find – a small fragment of Roman brick. Its distinctive flecked appearance, created by the use of ground-up brick fragments in its manufacture, enabled Mark to distinguish it from a modern brick and to identify it as Roman.

The tennis court site turned out to be relatively complex because of modern disturbance. This meant that, by the end of Day One, we had little evidence to show for our work. All the test pits were proving hard going, and it would take at least another four hours of excavation to yield results.

Day Two

Thanks to a local contact who had known the site in its early days, we discovered that we might be digging in the wrong place. If we intended to dig a trench where the sergeants' mess had once been, this had to be nearer the trees, approximately on top of what looked like a lavatory block. Another trench was begun in this area.

The test pits dug in the tennis court had started to produce Roman pottery, and geophysics had located more features at a deeper level.

After we had cleaned away the concrete rubble, our second trench in the sergeants' mess began to look more hopeful. After about three hours of excavation, we at last began to find substantial pieces of building material – not tesserae but large roofing tiles – which Mark identified as Roman. They had pointed bases and were impressively heavy, which made us realise what a strong and massive structure would have been needed to support a roof made from them. There appeared to be three colours: red, made from Pennant sandstone; a dull white, cut from limestone; and green, consisting of local greensand. This suggested a patterned green-

(Top) Two of the pointed Roman roofing tiles found in the second trench in the sergeants' mess. *(Mick Aston)* *(Middle)* A tile, found at Netheravon, which was once part of the flue of a hypocaust, the Roman system of central heating in which hot air from a furnace circulated beneath the raised ground floor. *(Mick Aston)* *(Above)* Computer reconstruction of a Roman flanged bowl, a fragment of which was found at Netheravon.

sand roof. Finally, from this trench we got our first tesserae – our first specific connection with Hawley's finds – and it gave us some cause for celebration at our Roman meal.

Day Three

We began the day by opening up a second trench on the coalyard site, and this soon produced more roof tiles in strong concentrations. Were we getting nearer to the centre of the villa or were we dealing with rubble that had accumulated around the edges? Lyndsay Allison-Jones, our Roman finds expert, was remarkably encouraging about the two tesserae we had discovered. One, small and red, was possibly from a room where wearing would have been lighter than the location of the second tesserae – a much chunkier yellow piece that, she felt, may have come from a corridor.

In the second sergeants' mess trench, Carenza was keen to find a wall or floor surface, but she faced a battle with the concentrated layers of Roman roof debris. No obvious foundations were apparent.

Phil and Mick became excited about what appeared to be the edge of a terrace in the second trench in the coal-yard. The villa would have been built on a platform terraced into the side of the hill overlooking the Avon, and even though the building may have been obliterated, the terraced edge might have survived. This at least gave us a boundary for the site – so could we find the elusive floor? Chris's latest geophysics readings turned out to be unhelpful. The tennis court pits contained Roman pottery but no building remains, and a strong feature that Chris had located turned out to be the remains of an air-raid shelter.

At this point, time was running out. With the trenches in the sergeants' mess and the coalyard revealing more roof debris that could be covering the villa's floor, it was a frustrating moment to end, but our three days were up. However, we had revealed many new elements on the villa site. The multi-coloured roofing material was probably the most important because it indicated that a large villa had been built here and approximately where it had stood. However, the results from the test pits had proved inconclusive, and many of us felt that these 1 metre by 1 metre pits were much less useful than we had originally considered.

Final thoughts from Mick

By Netheravon, I was able to walk on crutches and use a motorised wheel-chair, so I felt much more a part of what was going on.

I felt very pleased with our progress on the site. It was similar to the evaluation exercises carried out so often in present-day archaeology. While the 1-metre test pits were difficult, they usually enabled us to gain a general view of the site. The cumulative evidence allowed us to say a lot about the Roman buildings in detail, even though we did not find the exact site or the actual plan and layout of the villa.

Phil Harding *(left)* and a fellow excavator in the coalyard trench where the terrace edge was found. *(Mick Aston)*

TIME TEAM

SITE UPDATES

Not only does the work of TIME TEAM have a value of its own, but it can often spur on others to carry out further archaeological investigation. Here are updates on what has happened at sites explored by TIME TEAM in the last three series.

Much Wenlock. *(Mick Aston)*

SERIES 1

ATHELNEY & WEDMORE, SOMERSET

There was no excavation at the protected site at Athelney, but the investigation continues. After the TIME TEAM visit, the farmer 'unearthed' a number of artefacts (worked stone, tiles, pottery, etc.) from corners of his attic, and these are to be recorded, drawn and included in an article that will be published in the *Proceedings of the Somerset Archaeological and Natural History Society* in 1997.

Wedmore was a small farm site that, because of time constraints, was not included in the broadcast programme. The small evaluation trenches dug by TIME TEAM on an area deemed to have potential for housing development provided useful information for the archaeological context of the site. Development permission has since been given, but the buildings have been designed to protect the stratified archaeological remains (early medieval and possibly some Roman).

LLANGORSE, POWYS

Processing the material from every excavation season since 1989 is currently underway, and the artefacts from the TIME TEAM 'dig' are among those still under study. The shale ring has been conserved, and a preliminary assessment of the slags and metal-working evidence from the crannog has been completed. A bone comb from the site (not a TIME TEAM find) is on display at the National Museum in Cardiff. When the archaeological section there is next refurbished, Llangorse will be featured heavily in the Early Medieval Gallery as a unique and important site for Wales.

Every effort is being made to protect Llangorse into the next millennium. 1993 was the final year of work on the crannog, and the rest of the remains have been preserved for future investigation. Cadw, in conjunction with the Brecon Beacons National Park, has commissioned a report from engineers on how the erosion can be stopped to protect the site.

A joint publication by the National Museum and the University of Wales will be produced in due course. The results of the TIME TEAM work will be incorporated into this.

MUCH WENLOCK, SHROPSHIRE

The TIME TEAM investigation of property at 55 Sheinton Street, Much Wenlock identified a mid-13th-century house with a stone-built high end, or solar, and an aisled timber hall beyond, which may have been a guest house for visitors to the priory. Excavation extended past the kitchens and uncovered a rear yard and a large medieval cesspit. Digging continued after the TIME TEAM departed, and a well-preserved cobbled courtyard and drain leading up to the back wall of the medieval hall were also found. Further dendrochronological samples gave a more precise date for the building (AD 1254–90). One sample had nearly 400 rings, showing that this particular tree would have been planted around the time of King Alfred (AD 849–899).

Later that year, building work on the

Ribchester. *(Mick Aston)*

other side of Sheinton Street, which had been preceded by archaeological evaluation, revealed traces of lynchets (field boundaries) that may be Anglo-Saxon. This shows that Sheinton Street formed part of the Norman 'new town' built over farmland. Other work in the town in advance of redevelopment revealed plans of two more medieval halls, smaller frontage dwellings and backland occupation. These findings broadly confirm the model of the town's development that was originally suggested in the TIME TEAM programme.

All this work will, in the near future, form the basis of a study of the buildings and archaeology of the whole of Much Wenlock. The dendrochronology dates have been published in *Vernacular Architecture*. Reports on the archaeology of Much Wenlock are available in the Sites and Monuments Record, Shropshire County Council, Shire Hall, Shrewsbury.

RIBCHESTER, LANCASHIRE

There have been a number of evaluations and watching briefs in the village since the TIME TEAM excavations. Most of these have been on a small scale, but nearly all have produced interesting and significant archaeology that has added to the overall picture of the village in Roman times.

Results of the TIME TEAM's work will form part of a monograph by English Heritage on the Ribchester excavations, which is at present being reviewed and should be published sometime next year. Finds from the excavation are still being studied but will soon be sent to Ribchester Museum, doubling the size of their collection. They will join the current display of other archaeological finds from the village, which includes a cavalryman's tombstone from the banks of the River Ribble, as well as a replica of a cavalry parade helmet and various models of Roman soldiers and local tribes. The waterlogged nature of the excavation site means that there are a lot of very well-preserved leather and wooden objects, which are of particular interest.

SERIES 2

HYLTON CASTLE, SUNDERLAND

The development of Hylton Castle is a community initiative and an ongoing training programme for local people run by Sunderland City Council, aimed at elevating the status of the area and improving its amenities (including the building of an adventure playground and reconstructing some of the medieval gardens). Following TIME TEAM's involvement, an earthwork survey of the whole area has been completed, more documentary researches have been carried out and a design strategy for reconstructing the Elizabethan gardens has been produced. In addition, more trenches were excavated in a fairly sterile area to the west of the castle in preparation for footpaths and flowerbeds being laid out.

Prior to the city council developing a park within the grounds of the castle, a resistivity survey was carried out. The findings of this resulted in excavations, during which a medieval cobbled road right in the middle of the proposed play area was discovered. The council decided to redesign the playground to incorporate the ancient road, and a footpath now follows its course.

The resistivity survey also revealed a cobbled courtyard directly in front of the castle, and this too has been incorporated into the design of the park. Landscaping has been undertaken near the west front. The archaeologists carried out some small trial excavations in which they found some landscape features relating to the setting of the monument; the trenches contained no datable evidence but what was found looked as if it may date to the 18th century.

Last summer, an open day was held in front of Hylton Castle, including a medieval encampment, and there is the possibility of a similar weekend with educational workshops taking place in summer 1997. All this has stemmed from the interest generated by the TIME TEAM investigation. The castle is still in the care of English Heritage, which has carried out some conservation work (on beetle infestations and so on).

The report on the TIME TEAM excavations – with a contribution by Beric Morley, the team's buildings expert – is due to be submitted shortly either to the *Archaeological Journal* or *Archaeologia Aeliana*.

ISLAY, WESTERN ISLES

The stone-lined chamber on the top of the mound discovered during the TIME TEAM excavations was investigated further and found to contain animal bones, a fine Bronze Age flint arrowhead and a bone disc that may have been a threaded toy. It is possible that the chamber was a grave, but no trace of burials was found. The finds will be on display again at the Finlaggan Trust Visitors Centre in 1997, from Easter onwards.

Next to the chamber, the archaeologists found a 3-metre (9.8 ft) wide Bronze Age cairn. These cairns were known to have marked the burial places of important individuals, and there was evidence of a cremation burial here. It is possible that this may relate to a regional power centre in the medieval period.

Dr David Caldwell and his archaeological team will return to the site next summer, having enlisted the help of Army Engineers. Their plan is to build a dam in the loch between the two islets, which, it is hoped, will hold back the water from the midden that Tony helped excavate underwater. The archaeologists will then be able to excavate the midden deposits on dry land.

LAMBETH, LONDON

Lambeth Palace is planning to mount a permanent exhibition of some of the artefacts from the TIME TEAM garden excavations for visitors to see. A full archaeological report on investigations into Roman Lambeth and Westminster, including the TIME TEAM excavations, was published in *London Archaeology* (vol. 7, autumn 1995).

TOCKENHAM, WILTSHIRE

After the TIME TEAM's departure, local archaeologist Bryn Walters led a small excavation team to clarify the apsidal structure in the west wing of the Romano-British villa and to see exactly how much had survived. They immediately encountered the apse, locating it from the TIME TEAM geophysical survey. It appears to be polygonal, with five exterior sides and a semi-circular interior. It once contained a magnificent mosaic floor, constructed of very high-quality tesserae (mosaic pieces), which was totally destroyed 800 to 900 years ago. The large number of tesserae suggests that the mosaic would have covered the entire chamber; had it survived, it would have been the third largest mosaic-floored hall in England.

The excavators also found that the foundations had been completely robbed away, except for the very bottom courses of local oolitic stone; the rest was just backfilled rubble. This confirms the hypothesis that the walls were robbed out to build the earliest buildings in the village. Very little pottery was found.

A report of these excavations will be published in the forthcoming (1997) edition of the *Wiltshire Archaeological Magazine*, sponsored by Channel 4 Support Services.

WINTERBOURNE, WILTSHIRE

The material from the TIME TEAM excavations is being studied, together with that from excavations over the rest

(left) Islay. *(Mick Aston)*
(right) Winterbourne. *(Mick Aston)*

of the site. The report on the archaeology of the entire cemetery of about 80 burials, including those excavated by TIME TEAM, is currently being prepared for publication. This will appear in a future edition of the *Wiltshire Archaeological Magazine*, possibly in 1998.

The most significant outcome of the TIME TEAM excavations has been that the pond barrow, a last-minute discovery, has been scheduled and thus protected – the 61st example of these rare monuments.

The TIME TEAM excavation finds will be kept in Salisbury Museum, as will the archive. A selection of archaeological finds from earlier excavations at Winterbourne is on permanent display in the museum.

SERIES 3

BOLEIGH, CORNWALL

The tops of the stones from the courtyard house exposed by the TIME TEAM excavations are still just about visible in Jo May's garden next to the fogou. Jo has since written a book about his esoteric experiences living beside the fogou (*Fogou: A journey into the underworld*, published by Gothic Image). He favours the interpretation of a religious or ritual purpose for the fogou; TIME TEAM prefers to keep an open mind on fogous until firm evidence relating to their function is found.

The geophysics team had also carried out a survey at another fogou at Treveneague, which had been 'lost' for a century. The results of this were then tested by excavation to see whether the anomaly found did relate to the fogou. The trench showed that the fogou was still there, beneath a field of cabbages, but much of the building stone had been robbed out. Accurate information about its precise location can now be added to the Sites and Monuments Record.

The material from the fogou excavations has all been studied, and some of it is now being drawn for publication. A report on the TIME TEAM excavations will appear in a forthcoming issue of *Cornish Archaeology*.

Boleigh. *(Mick Aston)*

LAVENHAM, SUFFOLK

No further archaeological work has taken place on the site since the TIME TEAM excavations. A report on them was written for the Suffolk County Council Archaeological Service series. One of the brooches that was found has been conserved, ready for display, and the rest of the finds have been fully archived.

The TIME TEAM weekend had brought together Gilbert Burroughes, a local farmer and potter, and John Shepherd, a glass specialist from the Museum of London, and they are continuing the glass-furnace experiments started in Lavenham. They realised that they had learned many valuable lessons with the initial furnace and felt that they could make improvements in its efficiency. This summer at Gilbert's farm, they built a furnace of a slightly different design, though still keeping the model as close to surviving archaeological remains as possible, and rather than recycling more Roman glass, they used modern glass. To their delight, they found that they could reach a similar temperature without the use of bellows. This amazed Gilbert who, as a potter and a bit of an expert on furnaces, had believed that it was impossible. Next year, some glass-blowers will join them in an attempt to make precise replicas of Roman glass vessels using the same furnace.

Gilbert has also made some pieces of 'Samian' pottery and a mortarium, which are now in a teaching collection on exhibition in the Museum of London.

NAVAN, CO. ARMAGH

After TIME TEAM left Navan, Malachy Conway and his team continued the excavations at the site at Bally Doo for ten more days. The archaeologists found a vast amount of glass fragments dating to the early Christian period, including barley-sugar glass rods that gave evidence of glass-working or manufacture. Armagh is historically the ecclesiastical centre of Ulster, but Bally Doo is the only other site of this period in Northern Ireland to have been excavated. It was wonderful to have had the opportunity to investigate such a rare example, one that had not been destroyed by later buildings.

The geophysics team returned to Navan later in the year to do some more surveying work. Their results showed that the double ditch at Creeveroe extended more than half a kilometre further to the south, going up and over the hill and down the other side. This discovery had implications for Jim Mallory of Queen's University, Belfast, who has been carrying out annual excavations at Haughey's Fort. He didn't return to the entranceway discovered by TIME TEAM, but decided instead to look at the field to the south where he had been excavating these ditches for the previous two years.

The archaeologists were hoping to dig down to the three lines that were clearly visible on aerial photographs and had been confirmed on the geophysics printout, but they have had trouble locating some of them through excavation. They found the middle ditch, but the bottom ditch appears to have disappeared altogether, and what the archaeologists had thought was the upper ditch was actually one of its terminals. The excavation team are now looking for the other terminal to see where the ditch begins again, but so far, all they have found is an ever-widening gap. Two years ago, they found a late Bronze Age pin in a trench, and last summer, they discovered very small fragments of gold leaf from the occupation soil.

A prehistoric apple – still green after 3,000 years! – found at Haughey's Fort in 1991 is going to be DNA-tested at Oxford in the near future. This should give the archaeologists vital information as to whether apple cultivation was carried out at such an early date.

The main report on Dudley Waterman's excavations at Navan Fort between 1963 and 1971 is due to be published in 1997 as a Stationery Office monograph. The report on the excavations with TIME TEAM will be published in *Emania* in 1997.

STANTON HARCOURT, OXFORDSHIRE

Kate Scott and the Earth Watch volunteers have been very busy in the Oxfordshire gravel pit ever since TIME TEAM left. 1997 will be the final year for work at Stanton Harcourt as it will then be used as a landfill site as Kate and her teamalways knew. Following the precedent established during the TIME TEAM weekend, long parallel trenches have been dug right through the site using a digger, with finds recorded along the way, in an effort to get as big a picture of the site as possible before time runs out.

The archaeological team has excavated all through the past year and has continued to produce an amazing wealth of finds, including five stone tools from the river. One was a black flint tool for trimming, which showed very few signs of having been rolled in the prehistoric river. This suggests that it wasn't in the river for very long and hadn't travelled far. There have been many more finds from animal skeletons, including an entire bison skull complete with both horns, as well as some frustratingly enigmatic and as yet unidentified limb bones.

Stanton Harcourt. *(Mick Aston)*

It is a constant battle keeping up to date with the post-excavation work on so many finds, but research will continue for another few years after the end of the excavation itself, and this will be followed by publication of a report.

TEIGNMOUTH, DEVON

Following the broadcast of the TIME TEAM programme, there was a record increase in visitor numbers to Teignmouth Museum. No work was carried out on the Church Rocks shipwreck in 1996 as Chris Preece, the archaeologist, had left the project, but a new archaeologist has been assigned to the diving team and a three-week season is planned for 1997. Simon Burton is currently fund-raising to cover the costs of the work. A report on the TIME TEAM excavations has been sent to the Advisory Committee to Historic Wreck Sites at the Department of National Heritage.

TEMPLECOMBE, SOMERSET

Since the TIME TEAM investigation into the Templar preceptory at Templecombe, no further work has been carried out. The findings from the TIME TEAM excavation and surveys will, however, be useful to the Somerset archaeologists when considering planning applications, as they now know just where to expect to find the preceptory. Remains of very early buildings were found by archaeologists in the area identified by Carenza at the end of Day Three, behind the high medieval wall.

The report on the TIME TEAM excavations has been submitted to the *Proceedings of the Somerset Archaeological and Natural History Society*, for imminent publication.

Buildings expert Geoff Wilson has made a copy of a pot that was reconstructed from shards found during the three days, as well as a copy of one of the decorated tiles.

RESOURCES

GETTING INVOLVED

If you have been fascinated by the TIME TEAM series and this booklet and want to become more than an armchair archaeologist, there are a number of organisations that can provide advice and information.

COUNCIL FOR BRITISH ARCHAEOLOGY

A first step is to find out what is going on near you. The CBA has local and regional groups all over the country, and is the best source of information on every kind of archaeological subject. Members include professional archaeologists, local archaeological societies and museums and lots of interested amateurs. You, too, can become a member!

The CBA helps those who want to get involved in archaeology – in actual fieldwork, or by participating in meetings and events – by giving information, advice and practical support. Its regional organisations comprise a countrywide archaeologists' network.

The CBA also issues a popular news magazine called *British Archaeology*, the articles of which range right across the subject – from the Stone Age to the archaeology of the 20th century, from conservation to legislation, and from education to the latest discoveries and new ideas. The magazine contains campaigning editorials, and features and reviews by some of the best writers and thinkers in the field.

YOUNG ARCHAEOLOGISTS' CLUB

Part of the CBA, this is for people between the ages of 9 and 16 who take archaeology and the country's heritage seriously and also know how to have a good time. YAC members can take part in club activities through local branches around the country; they can also go on field study holidays and can even enter for the 'Young Archaeologist of the Year' award. Each member receives the club's quarterly magazine *Young Archaeologist* – packed with news about Britain and from correspondents abroad, as well as articles on things to do and places to go. The YAC president is Tony Robinson.

The address for both the CBA and the YAC is: Bowes Morrell House, 111 Walmgate, York YO1 2UA, tel: (01904) 671 417.

THE BRITISH ARCHAEOLOGICAL YEARBOOK

This up-to-date compendium of information about British archaeology includes a section on archaeology in education (at all levels), together with detailed listings of all archaeological organisations and a guide to archaeological resources available on the Internet. It is an invaluable source of information for anyone interested in archaeology, or wishing to get involved through study or practical experience. Published by the CBA, price £24.00.

CURRENT ARCHAEOLOGY

With six issues a year, this lively and popular colour magazine provides good coverage of news about recent finds, new books and topics of debate. Subscribers also get an extremely useful annual *Directory of British Archaeology*, full of names and addresses of archaeological organisations, and there are special offers for new subscribers. The annual subscription is £15.00, payable by cheque or credit card; for an extra £5.00 (£20.00 in all), you can get the latest three back issues plus the *Directory*. Contact Andrew Selkirk at: *Current Archaeology*, 9 Nassington Road, London NW3 2TX, tel/fax: (0171) 435 7517, e-mail: tsubs@archaeology.co.uk

ENGLISH HERITAGE EDUCATION SERVICE

In addition to caring for many monuments, English Heritage has a superb Education Service that exists to help teachers – at all levels – make full use of the historic environment. Visits to historic sites are a recommended part of the National Curriculum, and the Education Service offers guidance not only on sites' historical relevance, but also on the part that visits can play in subjects as varied as English, maths, science and geography. Schools can subscribe to a teachers' membership scheme, of which more details can be found in the leaflet *Windows on the Past*. Educational visits to sites are free.

To obtain *Windows on the Past*, the free booklets *Using the Historic Environment* and *Free Educational Visits* and the brochure *Resources* (which describes a host of educational publications and videos), write to: English Heritage Education Service, 429 Oxford Street, London W1R 2HD, tel: (0171) 973 3442, fax: (0171) 973 3443.

RECORDS AND ARCHIVES

The recording of historic monuments is the function of Royal Commissions that cover England, Scotland and Wales. Their role is to survey sites and landscapes, and to record standing buildings. In addition to producing a host of reference publications, they maintain libraries and archives, most of which are open to the public.

The Royal Commission on the Historical Monuments of England, home of the *National Monuments Record* (England's heritage archive), houses over seven million photographs of historic buildings, aerial photographs of archaeological sites, records of scheduled monuments and an extensive library. All are available to the public. For access, contact: National Monuments Record, Kemble Drive, Swindon SN2 2GZ, tel: (01793) 414 600.

Historic Scotland publishes two free leaflets concerning the archaeological record in Scotland: *Managing Scotland's Archaeological Heritage* and *Scheduled Ancient Monuments*. To receive a copy of either leaflet, contact: Historic Scotland, Longmore House, Salisbury Place, Edinburgh EH9 1SH, tel: (0131) 668 8600.

For Wales, contact **Cadw**, the Welsh Historic Monuments agency, at: Brunel House, 2 Fitzalan Road, Cardiff CF2 1UY, tel: (01222) 500 200. It can provide information for Welsh sites and monuments.

FURTHER READING

Oxbow Books in Oxford specialises in archaeology and carries an enormous stock of books. They also issue free lists of new publications every few months, and can supply all titles by post. Contact:
Oxbow Books
Park End Place, Oxford OX1 1HN
Tel: (01865) 241 249, fax: (01865) 794 449,
e-mail: oxbow@patrol.i-way.co.uk

CHANNEL 4 TELEVISION PUBLICATIONS

All of the following can be obtained by sending a cheque or postal order (payable to Channel 4 Television) to: TIME TEAM, PO Box 4000, London W5 2GH. Be sure to specify which titles you are ordering.

Time Team: An Archaeological A–Z
As the TIME TEAM whiz from one location to another, some of the team members may use terms that are unfamiliar to you. Or you may simply be interested in learning more about the techniques they employ to make sense of Britain's archaeological past. Either way, this booklet provides the answers. A4 booklet, illustrated in colour, 20 pages, 1994, £3.00.

The Time Team Reports
Full reports from the 1995 series on the possible location on Islay of the ancient Gaelic 'inauguration' ceremony of the Lords of the Isles; the parkland surrounding 14th-century Hylton Castle near Sunderland; the Romano-British villa found in a village in Wiltshire; areas on the Thames' banks where the Romans might have made their first crossing; and a 6th-century Saxon cemetery near Salisbury. Each report is accompanied by maps, photographs, computer reconstructions and a list of further reading. A4 booklet, illustrated in colour, 36 pages, 1995, £3.50.

Time Team 96: The site reports
Reports on Roman pottery in Suffolk, mammoths' tusks in Oxfordshire, the Knights Templar in Somerset, a rare Venetian wreck off Teignmouth in Devon, a prehistoric 'fogou' in Cornwall, and an ancient royal palace in Northern Ireland – with full details of what the team found and the archaeological methods used. Each report is accompanied by maps, photographs, computer reconstructions and a list of further reading, and there are also updates of sites visited in the two previous series. A4 booklet, illustrated in colour, 43 pages, 1996, £3.75.

ST MARY'S CITY, MARYLAND

Settlers on the Eastern Shore: British colonies in America 1607-1750, edited by John Scott, Facts on File, 1994, paperback, £7.95.
A concise history of the British colonisation of North America, from the first permanent colony at Jamestown, Virginia (established in 1607), the Plymouth Colony (1620) and the subsequent systematic colonisation of the entire Atlantic seaboard through to 1750.

Colonial America: A history 1607-1750 by R Middleton, Blackwells, 2nd ed. 1996, paperback, £15.99.
A slightly more difficult read, this work describes the history, both individually and collectively, of the 13 North American colonies established by Britain. It follows their progress up to the War of Independence, and examines aspects of colonial society such as the colonists' relations with Native Americans and the beginnings of slavery.

Historical Archaeology: A brief introduction by C E Orser and B M Fagan, HarperCollins, 1995, paperback, £8.99.
The archaeological study of people documented in recent history has expanded dramatically in the last few decades, especially in the United States. This book describes the basic principles, theory and global applications.

BIRMINGHAM

Companion to the Industrial Revolution by Clifford Lines, Facts on File, 1991, paperback, £8.95.
Comprises hundreds of A-Z entries, ranging in scope from a few descriptive words to mini-essays on the people, places and events that moulded one of the most important eras in British and, subsequently, world history.

The Industrial Revolution by Henry Dale and Rodney Dale, British Library, 1992, paperback, £4.95.
Shows how developments in the the harnessing of power and methods of transport transformed 18th- and 19th-century society, including the steam engine, the seed drill, the miners' safety lamp, iron-smelting, road-surfacing, canal engineering, steamboats and the railway.

Coins and Minting by Denis R Cooper, Shire, reprint 1996, paperback, £3.95.
Good introductory book to the early history of coinage and the development of production methods during the Renaissance and the Industrial Revolution.

LAUNCESTON, CORNWALL

The English Medieval Hospital 1050–1640 by Elizabeth Prescott, Seaby, 1992, paperback, £7.95 (Oxbow bargain price).
Examines the changing role of the hospital before and after the Black Death and gives a complete gazetteer of foundations of which something can be seen today.

Medieval Towns by John Schofield and Alan Vince, Leicester University Press, 1994, paperback, £9.95 (Oxbow bargain price).
Presents an overview of our knowledge of the medieval town - and urban and spatial interaction - in Britain between the 11th and 16th centuries, with chapters on such topics as houses, properties and streets, and churches, religious houses and cemeteries.

Studies in Crime: An introduction to forensic archaeology by John Hunter, Charlotte Roberts and Anthony Martin, Batsford, 1995, paperback, £25.00.
Archaeologists have made a very practical contribution to society in recent years by using paleoanthropological techniques to assist the police with their enquiries. This book discusses methods of searching for and locating buried remains and how those remains are recovered in order to maximise the potential evidence, (as with the skeleton found at Launceston).

GOVAN, GLASGOW

Govan and Its Early Medieval Sculpture, edited by Anna Ritchie, Sutton Publishing, 1994, hardback, £25.00.
Fourteen specialists write on different aspects of this old church. The subjects they cover include the Norse background to the hogback stones and the sculpture of the area, with comparisons with Irish sculptural art. A fairly scholarly book.

The following two books provide excellent coverage of this period of Scotland's past:

Viking Scotland by Anna Ritchie, Historic Scotland/Batsford, 1993, paperback, £15.99.
An examination of such aspects of Scottish history as where the Viking invaders came from, how much interaction they had with the Scots, and the longer-term effects of their settlement.

Picts, Gaels and Scots by Sally Foster, Historic Scotland/Batsford, 1996, paperback, £15.99.
A lively portrayal of Scotland's early inhabitants AD 600-1000, charting their economic, political and religious histories.

Glasgow, Clydeside and Stirling by Jack Stevenson, HMSO, 1995, paperback, £10.95.
Part of the 'Exploring Scotland's Heritage'

series, this well-illustrated book contains a wealth of fascinating information on the history and archaeology of the region, and also features a full-colour *Excursions* section with easy-to-follow trips.

MALTON, NORTH YORKSHIRE

Armourers by Matthias Pfaffenbichler, British Museum Press, 1992, paperback, £6.95.
Well-illustrated introduction to the communities of armourers that flourished in Europe, the individual armourers whose names and work are known, their companies or guilds and the processes involved in making and decorating armour.

Castles by Tom McNeill, Batsford, reprint 1996, paperback, £15.99.
Survey of information on the variety of castles in Britain and Ireland, and on why they were built where they were, who built them, how they were adapted to seige warfare, and so on.

English Castles: A guide by counties by Adrian Pettifer, Boydell, 1995, hardback, £25.00.
A comprehensive yet concise guide to all medieval English castles of which something can be seen today. Over 500 entries, grouped in traditional county order, each with a brief history and description of the site.

The Tudor and Jacobean Country House: A building history by Malcolm Airs, Sutton Publishing, 1995, hardback, £18.99.
The English country house was one of the most exciting developments of the 16th century. This book explores how they were designed and built – from the choice of site and involvement of the patrons to the contributions of the craftsmen and the daily lives of the labourers.

NETHERAVON, WILTSHIRE

Roman Britain by T W Potter, British Museum Press, 1983, paperback, £6.95.
The four centuries during which the Roman presence in Britain rose, flourished and declined changed every aspect of life: industry, trade, government, the arts and learning. This book gives an illustrated outline of the period.

Roman Villas by David E Johnston, Shire, 4th ed. 1994, paperback, £3.95.
An excellent guide to the archaeology of villas, their architecture and their role in the life of Roman Britain as centres for agricultural production.

Roman Villas and the Countryside by Guy de la Bédoyère, Batsford, 1993, paperback, £15.99.
A more detailed study that places the villas firmly in the context of the wider landscape and of their place in the overall economy of Roman Britain.

A Taste of Ancient Rome by Ilaria Gozzini Giacosa, University of Chicago Press, 1992, paperback, £13.50.
More than 200 recipes from Ancient Rome are updated here for the modern chef, including everything from sauces, soups and appetisers to meat, fish, vegetables and desserts. Includes an introduction to the history of banqueting in Ancient Rome, as well as everyday menus of Roman families.

Published in 1996 by Channel 4 Television
124 Horseferry Road, London SW1P 2TX

Produced by Broadcasting Support Services to accompany TIME TEAM 4
(a Video Text Communications production for Channel 4, in association with Diverse Production), first shown on Channel 4 in January–February 1997

Writer: Tim Taylor Archaeological consultant: Mick Aston Site Updates: Victoria Batten
Editor: Paula Snyder Editorial consultant: Nancy Duin
Design: Neil Dell/9th Planet Maps and Illustrations: Nick Pearson Computer Reconstruction: Creative TV Facilities Printer: Windsor Print Production Ltd
Distributed by Broadcasting Support Services

Broadcasting Support Services provides follow-up services for viewers and listeners and runs long-term helplines.

BSS

Channel 4 Television would like to thank the following for their help in producing this booklet: Susan Bain, Mark Corney, Cornwall County Council Archaeology Unit, George Demidowicz, Steve Driscoll, Nick Johnston, Suzanne Lavery, Henry Miller, Beric Morley, Ryedale Folk Museum Hutton-le-Hole, N Yorks), Trust for Wessex Archaeology Unit. Channel 4 would also like to acknowledge Kevin Greene's Archaeology:An introduction (Batsford, 1983, rev. ed. 1995) as a source for some of the diagrams in this booklet.

To help viewers follow up the issues raised by programmes, Channel 4 publishes a wide range of booklets, factsheets and edited transcripts, as well as organising telephone support services. You can also access Channel 4 programme support on the Internet:
http://www.channel4.com

Channel 4's teletext service 4-Tel also contains regularly updated information for viewers. To access 4-Tel: make sure that your television is tuned to Channel 4, press the text button, then enter the number of the page you want to access. The 4-Tel index is on page 300. Details of Channel 4 programme support, including helplines and booklets, appear on page 340.

If you want to express your opinion on *any* television programme, not just those you see on Channel 4, contact:
Right to Reply
Channel 4 Television, 124 Horseferry Road, London SW1P 2TX
Tel: (0171) 306 8582 Fax: (0171) 306 8373
e-mail: right2reply@channel4.co.uk

For further copies, please send a cheque or postal order (made payable to Channel 4 Television) for £4.00 (including postage & packing) to:
TIME TEAM 97
PO Box 4000, London W5 2GH or Cardiff CF5 2XT

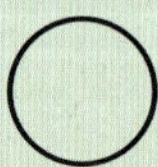
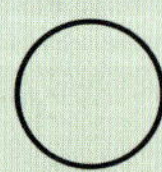
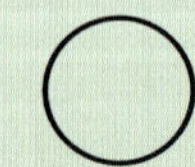